MAHMUT NEDIM

DANCE OF SHIVA

Metaphysics of Life and Love

Translated to English by

Leila Faraday

To my father, who always faced life with a song...

And to those who sing

and dance...

About the author :

The author was born in a central Anatolian town which was demoted from the status of province, when it declined to vote for the ruling party of the time, but was later reinstated to its former standing. While torn by the decision between a future in metallurgical engineering or psychiatry, his pursuit of the school heartthrob led him to apply for the Civil Service. In the end, the object of his desires failed to obtain enough points to register herself. But in front of the student registry on his first day at college, the author met another fellow student with whom he still maintains a close friendship.

After completing his education there, his dreams of working in film came to nothing but he went on to become a successful banker. During his childhood, he thought that he would die before seeing Istanbul and the sea. His poignant memories of those days include shouting out, 'Say hello to my dad!', with his local friends whenever an airplane flew over, even though they all knew it was nonsense, as well as sitting in questioning silence when fish was served for dinner, believing that if he drank water afterwards, the creature would come alive in his stomach.

He wrote his first book, 'Basit Hayat Kuralları' (Simple Rules of Life) after resigning from his job, following which he returned to his former company albeit in a different role. Later, he once again resigned from his job to produce the book in your hand, but this time the thereafter is unknown. Life is constantly offering up surprises and has been doing so for 14 billion years. This is as true for the author as for anyone.

AT THE BEGINNING

When I was a child, the story of the genie that appeared from the lamp was one of the tales that most caught my imagination. Although the story did not quite fit with my logical reasoning, it was as if my existence was a witness to its veracity, and I was always more interested in the genie rather than Aladdin. Likewise with Rapunzel, I remember how enchanted I was by the magic of the book. I read it over and over again, maybe a thousand times.

As life comes at us, reflected in a thousand and one forms by the mirrors of the universe, people are naturally curious about its initial, original form. The joys and sorrows that give substance to the meaning of life seem to belong to us, but we can never be quite sure; perhaps they are unexpected guests that have come to us from far off places. It is as if the known and the unknown walk arm in arm through our cycle of birth and death.

With this book, you will embark on a journey from the world of subatomic particles towards the meaning of love, at times accompanied by the light of science and at times by emotional responses. This is a 14-billion year journey that started in a ball of fire with the Big Bang. What this means is that within the universe, there is a system and force that is outside the laws of physics. As for the physicists, even they began to talk about God once they gained a greater understanding of the universe. In all probability, it will not be long before they are also talking about love.

However, in our search for well-being and love, life's greatest impulses, it is impossible not to wonder whether or not there is a cosmic function that will give us some answers. There must be; but unfortunately some of life's secrets cannot be perceived by a simple process of learning and that is why we probably need a different type of perception that can go beyond our consciousness. If there is one thing Zen Buddhists must know, it is that they can only take you closer to the threshold of knowledge and leave you there. From there on, it is down to you how much you can open up your perception.

In any case, Love is not sex and kissing.
Dreams of happiness? No, it never was...

Perhaps love is the tinkle that comes with the first touch of your tiny hand on a huge, ponderous bell, or the speck of light that slips into your eyes. Perhaps it is the voice that tells you to stay when you are about to go... The impulse that propels you to someone's side because you miss them. In other words, we don't understand exactly what love is. In fact, it is a kind of magic charm. A charm chiselled into the foundation stone of life. So what is this charm?

CHAPTERS

LOVE

I might not have been head over heels in love, but I was besotted - that's for sure. There were other possibilities for me at the time, but she was the important one. We were working at the same place. At almost every midday break, I would dodge the others and go for lunch with her. We loved talking together with a passion and she frequently referred to how much she valued me, complaining,

'Why can't I find a lover like you?'

Despite that, we never became lovers. Rather than choosing me, she always had unhappy relationships with footloose drifters. After every break-up, her pain would spill out across the table between us as she asked what my common sense was telling me about it all.

I don't know why I was so passionate about her out of all the young, beautiful women around me. Although she was regretful, for some reason she always shot wide of the mark when it came to me, her bullets glancing off on a tangent to find others. We both meandered around each other without ever coming together. We were like planets unable to change our course, approaching each other's orbit then distancing ourselves again after a set time.

Now, when I look at the past, I can see that in all our romances, we become inexplicably attached to each other and then, inexplicably again, the ties slacken. For example, what does it mean to get bored? What feeds this boredom? Why is it that while everything seems to be going well, we get fed up and separate? Love either strikes or doesn't strike, with no criterion, timescale or foundation. We have never been able to tell where, when and how it would strike and sometimes it skips right over the people who most deserve our love, enslaving us instead to those who we should loathe.

In the end, your choice falls, not on the level-headed man or woman who loves you, but someone else who turns life into a prison. But it wasn't always that way. At one time, your life together was full of enthusiasm and you held each other passionately. Is there any power in this huge universe that can separate two bodies and souls that are locked together in love? Even if death comes between them, they still cling to each other; if you empty every bullet in your magazine into their bodies, instead of holding their hands over their own wounds, their fingers will reach out towards each other. This is not a random, emotional flood that recurs now and again, or a treatable illness. It is a rapture that has been repeated throughout human history in every corner of the world. The fascinating thing is that even if most of the time it brings us pain, we all still pursue it.

The joining together and subsequent experience are always the same - like a law of physics. The souls join together inside these two idolized bodies and become at one with the universe in a huge gala firework display. The whole world is melted into their bodies, which beat with one heart in the cosmic darkness. A while later, the lovers slowly regain awareness of their own existence and begin to ask themselves what happened, as if they are waking after a long dream. Their lives return to a familiar path. They each resume their individual identity.

It is as if the emotions evoked by love move between us like radio waves. Suddenly, we recoil as if something has hit us, or shudder as if a spark has flown inside us. The waves pervade our bodies and souls like the ripples of a stone thrown into water. To be able to relive it again and again, we savour the heavenly moment, drop by drop.

Sometimes an arrow plants itself deep in our heart. We burn inside. A dark pain descends over our existence. Some part of us is bleeding, but we cannot tell if it is blood that is seeping out or our soul.

Maybe all of this is our existence, scorched by the breath of the Big Bang - the magic spell of 14 billion years ago, the secret of the charm that started all existence, engraved into life's codes. Could it be that love is the act of the scattered particles, which sought each other out after the small core exploded, as they still attempt to lock together even 14 billion years later? Is love the soul of every subatomic particle? Is that the explanation for love's fervour and resistance? Right or wrong, just or unjust – does love mean not leaving each other for any reason and not going back? Why is it that love always wants to be as one and, for as long as it stays within these bodies, never wants to depart in any way? Or is love the process by which electrons and their antiparticle, positrons, shining with their two beams of light, are annihilated when they collide?

When Paul Dirac was awarded the Noble Prize in 1933 for his discoveries relating to electron-positron collision, he undoubtedly was not thinking about love. Those granting the award must certainly not have had that in mind. But what does this change? Does the transformation of electrons and positrons into light energy (photons), leaving behind their individual existences when they collide, remind you of something else? Is it because they are not born from a human mother or father that their annihilation and light is not associated with the human legend called love? The Noble Prize for literature and the Oscar Awards also always appear to gravitate towards expositions on love and the reflections of its spirit, despite the official justification given for the winners. No matter how much Boris Pasternak's Dr Zhivago is lauded for its opposition to the Soviet regime, who would deny that it was the portrayal of an anguished love eclipsing the suffering of the era that earned it a Nobel Prize?

Whatever is said about the roots of Pablo Neruda and the South American people coming together far under the surface, is there anyone who would refute that 'Twenty Love Poems and a Song of Despair' and his 'love sonnets' are deserving holders of the Nobel Prize? Love is the most striking global phenomenon there is, happening at every moment in every corner of the world. Say what you like, love wafts around us as a single force dominating our existence, passing from one body to the next through emotional transmission.

The sensation called emotion, in which we carry love, is perhaps a letter carried in the hands of a courier, and when we perceive it, we are opening the door to this new guest. You are overwhelmed by the sight of them, the words they write or the sound of their voice. As well as informing us of our feelings, this emotion also emboldens us with an inner strength. We might talk about the strength of our emotions, but for some reason, we don't really want to believe that they are a force of their own or have any such power...

You were washing vegetables in the kitchen, when little Volkan cried out,

'Mum, my head! My head!'

When the words 'mum' and 'my head' reached your ears, how did you feel? Wasn't it as if your ear had been punctured with a knife? Were you aware of the force of strength behind you as you flew into the kitchen? What was it that propelled you like a rocket? As you are ambling down a dark street with your lover, three men block the path in front of you, demanding,

'Give us the woman!'

Imagine the chemical reactions that start to kick in when you hear those words - and the strength that starts to course through your body.

Emotion might well be an additional force to the four universal forces (electromagnetic, gravitational force etc.), or perhaps a version of these forces... But if there is one known reality, it is that emotion carries a force of its own. In the pages to come, we look for the roots of numerous behaviours we have experienced or adopted as if they are a standard part of our daily life, and maybe we will unearth them in the most unexpected places, with the same joy as when unearthing artichokes or potatoes in the garden.

In this vein, it could be said that the inspirational idea behind this book is to search for the root of love, well-being and other types of behaviour, in the language of the universe - to chase behind the reflections of the core that opened out with the big bang 14 billion years ago, as we see it reflected in our lives today. We will trace our family tree back 14 billion years as if we are researching our family heritage, not just looking at love, but also hate, friendship, journeys, recuperation, starting a family, growing up, success, affluence, happiness, death - in summary, why we live life the way we do.

Questioning is the first step to learning and learning is the first rung on the ladder of command. Is there a way to control our lives in the same way that the universe self-created and gave itself a direction? Is there a path to achieving love, comfort, health and beauty? After all, aren't we made of the same clay as the cosmos, so why shouldn't there be? We should be able to manage it just as well as the cosmos; it should be enough that the cosmos can direct its own life. That being the case, rather than writing the secret recipes of love and success, perhaps it would be better to stand back from the light of life to enable everyone to find their own way in this labyrinth. Without indulging in any esoteric riddles, we will move forward by being aware that the necessary information is already in front of us, pulling the oars of the boat with our own hands. Even if our boat sometimes gets lost in the rapids of this tropical forest through which all the information of life gushes, we know that the place where we will end up is where we need to be and that it is not possible to be truly lost in the universe, no matter how bewildered we may feel at times.

That day was the first day. It was as if the schools has opened and as always it seemed too soon. The first day...

EXISTENCE

As existence suddenly transformed into hell, a heat never previously experienced and never to be felt again was baking everywhere in a storm cloud. As the fireball grew and spread, someone screamed,

'The forgotten core has exploded! We're heading for disaster! Run!'

The scientists would appear on television saying,

'Friends, you are mistaken. Don't see it as the Big Bang we said we would welcome with open arms - there was nothing there to explode. It's the entity of God that is expanding and you thought it was an explosion.'

Just at that moment, someone sitting quietly in the back row, wracked with the fear of still not comprehending what was going on, would interject with the secret question,

'So does that mean that God has created his own hell?'

These baleful words would whip up an icy wind. Sometimes it happens like that, like when a small child easily grasps something beyond their experience without any prior information.

Divine matters are always isolated in our public lives. Just as high voltage lines must not be touched, so too are these subjects forbidden for bare hands. It is not known where the topic will take us, how deep it will go and what will be unearthed, and likewise, part of the curtain cannot be opened. Our delving into the divine can be likened to reading a script in our hands in a theatre in which the curtains are down, and not to question or wonder what is going on behind them or take one step forward. The script being read is the script approved by official religious authorities and the deepest, most comprehensive censors in the whole world are related to religion. It's for this reason that the beliefs of Muslim Sufis are removed from official religious teaching and they are sometimes politely referred to as 'possessed'. Christian Cathars were also persecuted and burnt by the church.

But sometimes, a child or one of the possessed peeks under a corner of the curtain when people are least expecting it. As a white-haired woman sitting at the end of the front row clinches an unstitched part of her skirt hem under her knees to keep it hidden from the cameras, she mutters to herself, 'How strange that we are all in it...'

So much time has passed from that time until the present day... We have pretty much forgotten everything.

5,110,000,000,000th day.

Vietnamese and Palestinian children have gone through similar excitement and horror when an aircraft bomb buried in the ground suddenly exploded or when the hot wind burnt their skin in Hiroshima.

The reason I am mentioning these is that perhaps fire and horror are not foreign concepts for us, because our core originated from them, and that may be why we have never found them particularly strange. Even the children of Hiroshima and Vietnam disappeared after fading away in a few snapshots and poems. But fires and exploding bombs have always been within us, and throughout our history we have constantly sought new justifications and situations in which to try them out again. Almost every war has been an orgy of horror into which we have willingly plunged. No matter how deep the pain, we have always been there, eagerly pursuing the cause, fighting on the front and dropping the bombs. What was the source of the wave that passed through us, the trance that we were unaware of, or didn't want to be aware of as we dropped napalm on the villages? The fireball is always within us... We frequently speak about being in hell, even in jokes. Heaven is a far-off possibility for all of us, and the guard waiting at hell's gates is far more close and familiar to us than the angels of heaven.

If there had been people around and they were able to withstand the heat and pressure, the first day might have resembled the scenario described above in a somewhat caricatured manner. In the first second, even one trillion degrees centigrade was a tiny figure for the universe. Hell is hell when it is inhabited by people. As the first tick-tock of time began with the big bang, it would be another 14 billion years before the sexton would pull the ropes of the bell tower to announce the arrival of humans on the scene. It's as if preparations for our arrival began from that moment on. Hell had been created, but heaven was not yet in existence. In the meantime, 10 billion years passed. On one hand, a fireball of one trillion degrees centigrade was growing and on the other hand it was cooling, until eventually a scattered hot cloud significantly cooled and densified, turning into Earth, which made the existence of heaven possible.

In truth, we do not know why the universe created itself. One possibility is that it was curious and wanted to look inside itself. But you might ask, 'Why should it wonder about itself? Is it a living thing?' To belittle the universe, the source of our very being and life itself, and downgrade it to the class of soil and stone is probably a logic peculiar to the human race alone. It's perfectly understandable that the communication and comprehension skills of our brains, which have spent two million years inside our skulls yet only learned how to write 5,000 years ago, should still be far from a deeper perception of the essence of the universe and its unique language, disregarding and devaluing that which we see but do not understand.

Therefore, it's right to consider that this question has not been asked. Bearing that in mind, even the cosmic essence cannot be freed from curiosity, particularly when it comes to its very existence. We do know one thing: the cosmos strived to turn back all its energy and rapidly spreading mass, as if it regretted what it had done. At the end of this conflict, as Einstein put it, the universe began to warp.

DISTORTION

Cosmic formations are incredibly new additions to our knowledge banks. Even the distorted structure of the universe was only discovered at the start of the 20th century by a scientist called Einstein. Everything that exists affects life's shape, thwarting and distorting our plans. That's why calculations made at home don't seem to work out at the market and why God looks at and laughs at the plans people make. As the proverb says, there is no escaping destiny, and even the road you traverse towards your target through your own volition can be contorted and change direction.

Physical mass is the most unique and familiar form of existence, and the distortion that results from gravitational force is a reflection of this mass. Put in another context, existence reflects will. Gravitation and will are like two wings of the same mechanism and can only originate from mass. Beginnings form with a magic originating from the cosmos, which even the universe cannot resist. Almost 14 billion years have passed since the first day, and our Earth, which densified and hardened when it was a light cloud, is only four billion years old. It is only two million years ago that our ancestors stood up on two feet on our small planet earth and we have only been surviving on two feet for one and a half million years. It was about 500,000 years ago that we learnt how to throw sharp stones at other creatures. We only managed to figure out how to produce part of our food supply with agriculture 10,000 years ago. Let's not ponder too much on what kept us busy in the intervening 500,000 years - I have no wish to dishonour our ancestors. I might add that it was just 5,000 years ago that we figured out how to read and write.

The history of the most crucial tools of our civilisation goes back 200,000 years. Sadly, we only discovered that time was a dimension 14 billion years after it had started - 200,000 years after homosapiens and 10,000 years after we began to engage in agriculture. On the face of it, we cannot be considered that smart. Most of the time, our attempts to make judgements about the 14-billion-year cosmic process with a consciousness shaped by a mere 60-70 years of life are comical; but, not to worry, ignorance is the mother of bravery. On the other hand, if we look back, not just 30-40,000 years, but billions of years ago to the point at which we started out, not as humans but as a part of cosmic existence, it is impossible not to appreciate the storms we have weathered and the fact that we are beings that have even been through a one trillion degrees centigrade fireball. When we look at the foundation stones of our life from this point of view, it is apparent that cosmic laws are not so confused and multifarious after all.

In fact, there are altogether four universal forces discovered by physicists. Two of them are gravitational force and electromagnetic force. The others are called strong force and weak force. Everything under the celestial sphere moves with these four forces. Four forces have managed the universe for billions of years, without making one mistake. If we stop behaving like creatures that do not like the shell they have emerged from, we can accept that these four forces are directing us and look at how they are actually doing it. When looking from this angle, we become aware of how simple life actually is and how we fail to see many things that we actually know. It might surprise us to see that the laws of physics are the foundation for our societal laws. When it comes to our personal relations, can we argue with the fact that, inside the completeness of cosmic existence, at the root of every individual decision is the presence of a generic law.

BEGINNING

Is beginning easy? Decision and action...Removing the sword from its scabbard...thrusting it into the heart...telling someone you love them...baring your body and soul in front of another to make love...leaving someone. The first move is always hard. All vehicles use their greatest power when setting out - the first rotation of the wheel or the first elevation of the aircraft's nose. When we start out on a new road, other things keep popping up in our way, attempting to stop us in our tracks. Then we say, 'Maybe later, but not now.' Some might say, 'Tomorrow...' while others say, 'Let's think about it a bit more.'

Even when we start to read a book, a myriad of alternatives appear before us - from making a sandwich, phoning a few friends or going to the shop to buy milk. All things try to obstruct our will and intended actions. Maybe we do it ourselves too...No matter how much the dream of a new job, new partner or new house excites you, the minute you spring into action, your stomach tightens and you feel the need to apply the brakes. Then, while we wait tensely, unable to set out along the road and convincing ourselves that it is not yet the right time, something suddenly happens; the missing piece falls into place and we start to move in a new direction. We still don't know who puts that piece into place, but it is at this moment that the long awaited movement we have almost given up on begins.

Beginning is to crown movement with a new direction. It includes saying no as well as yes. For example, how many reasons do you have for leaving your wife, husband or lover? How many times were you scorched with regret?

You know that you need to escape from the relationship, but what can you do when your feet just won't take you there? As if your whole life is conspiring to stop you, every time you find something to justify waiting and postponing your decision. Sometimes months, even years, pass. Life has no standard timetable.

It could be that all these obstacles are a reminder to our soul that beginning is an act of no-return. We ought to know this from way back, because we all went through the very first beginning, the Big Bang, together. At that time, we were profoundly close to everything in existence and could have stretched out our arm to embrace the whole cosmos. Even more, at the outset of the first second, the furthest corner of the universe was 10-35 metres (1 Planck length) away from us: something like 0,000.000.000.000.000.000.000.000.000.000.000.001 meters - such close proximity to all the limits of existence and so completely ensconced in each other that we must know all the secrets of existence.

Nevertheless, we need to accept that remembering the first day now (the Big Bang) is fraught with difficulties due to the 14-billion-year gap in between. In fact, the first day was so spontaneous that the workings of the ensuing period melted into cosmic movement and became invisible. That is why the question of where, why and how something started in that way seems to us to be the most difficult, complex and mystical question. The cosmos is a vast enchanted sea inside which all magic is formed. Even fantastical tales are a reflection of cosmic laws: glasses that never fill and bottles that never empty are alien to our fixed assumptions, but children, whose perceptions are still unnarrowed by daily life, accept them.

That could be why astrology came about. When the obfuscated knowledge of everyday life cannot explain the secret of the new beginnings flowing before us, we should turn our eyes to the sky. Much as it may seem that searching for answers above is the kind of naive perception associated with primitive people, it originates from instincts deep within us. However, our needs on this subject are not quite fulfilled by astrology. Astrology is not concerned with future events in our life, but rather its predispositions. The beginnings are down to us. It can identify the existence of tendencies predisposing us to new beginnings, but it does not shed light on the reasons for these events and tendencies. Astrology is something of a method contained in a sealed box; whilst we do not fully understand it, it provides answers to some of our questions.

As for beginning, it is a magic charm about which we have no knowledge. Beginning means the first few steps we take through the gates that life keeps tightly closed with a taut spring. Beginning is to open one of these trillions of gates. Every day, every moment, new gates are forming across the cosmos in such great numbers as to make trillions seem infinitesimal and trillions of these will turn into solid walls that will never be opened again. Despite the difficulty of opening these gates secured by a taut spring, as soon as they open the magic happens, allowing a new direction of life to flow in front of us. Then it is up to you whether or not to go with the flow. When you surrender your existence to the flow, you think to yourself, 'If I had known it would be like this, I would not have been so hesitant.'

Even actors who have been on the stage for over 30 years of their lives have doubts every time they walk onto the stage. They approach tentatively, tense and afraid, as if someone might suddenly pull the floor from under their feet. Every play is a new beginning for life and with every new beginning comes tension. In fact, motion would not be possible without this tension. But why does tension propel movement? It might not have been that way. Why does pressure lead to explosion? Quite the opposite might be true. Still, if that is the way things are, then it is something unique to our universe, in which the essence of motion is force and force is the abracadabra of the universe.

Just as in the fable of Nasreddin Hoca and the whistle, or the proverb, 'he who pays the piper calls the tune', the universe could not engender any motion at all without force (tension). Just think what a nightmare you go through when you are first about to admit that you love someone - like a sailor holding onto the mast for dear life, your hand grips the pen so tightly it almost breaks. Maybe you are writing to your old colleague, with whom you have discussed all manner of topics and shared your anxieties for nigh on ten years. Or perhaps it's the person you have seen every morning for several years at the ferry quay on your way to work, greeting them with 'good morning' but unable to decide for months what the next word might be?

Beginning is in fact the end of chaos - trapped, clotted energies released by the swishing sword of Alexander the Great. Beyond that, if we want to illuminate the magic charm of beginning, we first need to unravel the spell of the Big Bang. Every detail of the Big Bang casts a light on the inner forces and mechanisms of beginning. When you push a door, it opens, and the passage waits for your first step. Now is the time for beginning and you must make that step. If you do not make a start, nothing else will follow. The inner quiver of desire is now ready to turn into a decisive step.

We were two disparate people who both travelled to work every morning on the 8 a.m. ferry. The quay was never that busy because our stop was the first on the circular route. Although we didn't know each other's names and exchanged but a few greetings, we knew where each of us always sat. Even when we eventually recognised each other, we never let on. We waited in the passenger lounge for the ferry to approach the quay, before boarding calmly, with no pushing or shoving, and making way for each other in unstated acquiescence to our secret acquaintance. Everyone on the ferry had a distinct identity: there were those who read books and newspapers, and those who gazed at the shorefront houses throughout the whole journey. Although we had gathered significant information about our fellow travellers during the many journeys, for some reason or other it was forbidden to speak or enter one another's personal space and there were just a few people who acknowledged each other with a faint smile.

Almost two years passed as I wondered how I could break the ice with her. Every morning, out of the corner of my eye I would try to weigh up whether or not she was interested in me, but I could discern nothing from her behaviour. She was completely shut off from the outside world. Seemingly unaware of my presence, her eyes generally fixed on empty spaces, as if she was warning anyone off talking to her, and I did not have the courage to try and assail this barrier. In some periods of their life, people are stuck at the foot of a brick wall. They have no idea what to do, and even when jostled by an inner voice telling them to act, they are still unable to take the next step. Until the time comes...

That morning, as fine drops of rain mixed in with the cold wind, piercing the skin like a razor, we were the first to arrive at the quay. The automatic ticket barrier would neither accept our tokens nor open. After she had tried a few times with no success, I suggested she jumped in through the side of the barrier. We jumped inside together. Seeing our dishevelled state, the young official smiled and said, 'It's on us today!' That was the moment when our gate opened, and we took our first steps into one another. Having spent months trying to think up a first sentence, the cosmic gate lock had transformed into the lock of the barrier in front of us, prompting the magical sentence to arrive of its own accord to activate the key.

She smiled so beautifully as she was speaking, suddenly seeming like a different person. It was like a smile hidden inside an oyster in the depths of the sea. At that moment, I thought of Venus, who was born from the Mediterranean ocean spume. A fragile ingenue who perhaps could not be touched for fear of causing hurt, and hence her crystal soul was hidden away in a cold, dense layer of ice. Sometimes, our inner knots unravel and the locks of our inner prison are opened by a key that has taken shape inside our desires. We haven't solved the magic of existence, but still we must believe in it. However much we sidle closer to it, it will blow its soul away by that much again. This magic is the core of existence and consequently of the universe itself. Although in all likelihood, it is something other than magic, we should have no qualms in referring to it as magic for now. The important thing is to name it, for now...

The magic exists inside life, but a part of life that is foreign to us. For every beginning there is a spell - either good or bad. And this is what astrologists endeavour to discover. They seek the inner trembles of birth and all kinds of beginnings in the sky. We all habitually wish good luck on the birth of a child, but we also do it just as much for any new beginning - a book launched onto the market or the opening of a new company. Although some find this behaviour somewhat ridiculous because it doesn't fit within the limits of positive sciences, strangely enough few of us hold back from wishing it with the utmost sincerity. Why? Of course, we are fully aware that simply wishing a company good luck will not guarantee its success, so why do we give in to such absurdities?

If we don't open out souls to the magic of existence, we will certainly see nothing but absurd scenarios. In that case, it means the time has come for us to open our souls in the direction of the deep tremor we call the magic of the universe.

THE CHARM OF NOTHINGNESS

At one time, there was neither a universe, nor its three dimensions and time. Maybe there was also nothing there to explode. As long as there was no existence and no dimensions, there could be nothing to explode and scatter. Physicists may not be able to give a clear answer to the question, ' What was there at the beginning?' but they say they know what happened after the initial moment of the beginning. We can't even imagine what was there prior to that moment, because if there was no time and space, there could be no before or after. The intense squeezing of a non-existent dimension is perhaps the first and most important magic of existence (Contemporary knowledge tells us that without dimensions, there can be no squeezing. Unfortunately, we do not yet have any concept to understand this kind of squeezing.) Perhaps children are the only ones who understand the opening refrain of fairy tales, 'Once upon a time', shaped as it is with a perception outside of our cultural norms.

In short, the universe may have been smaller than a single atom. Whatever density would emerge from squeezing the universe's current volume of density into that dimension, we can comfortably say that it would have been the same then. This is because physicists state that the universe was closed and from that moment up until the present, nothing could enter from outside. Everything that is in the firmament now: stars, nebula, galaxies, all kinds of matter and antimatter were squeezed into that tiny genie's lamp. Yes, we have hit the nail on the head - it was squeezed incredibly tightly and we can comfortably say that the process that would start off cosmic life was connected to the mechanism applying the squeeze.

Accordingly, if we want to start anything, we can do so by mimicking the cosmic process - squeeze and wait. Squeeze and squeeze again... Keep at it without losing hope and system will eventually answer us, perhaps in the form of an explosion or perhaps something else, but there will definitely be a response. If we can even explode nothingness to make a huge universe, why then shouldn't we be able to form new and important processes from a few facets of our everyday lives. That is the spell... And we need neither abracadabra mantras or magicians to bring it upon us. You will see that it is much easier to find the spell of life within the laws of physics. You can be your own magician. If you don't manage to become a magician, this short hypothesis should at least make you competent to work as an interrogator for secret services. I can guarantee that this methodology will guarantee your success there. In any case, they know this secret themselves.

You don't believe it...You're thinking that it can't be that simple. How could the spell of existence be compacted into a one-line hypothesis in this cheap book? Well, you are right. There is nothing in this book; it is simply a prompt for where to look. Unfortunately, the author is not the genie of the lamp, but he does think he has seen the genie and in the depths of his heart, a gnome is pointing his finger and saying, ' The genie of the lamb is over there...' The genie is still wandering among physicists. If the laws of physics correspond to the laws of life, why do we seek other laws and sources? We live in the home of Lady Universe and at the same time we are an inseparable part of it, so we shouldn't need anything but the laws of the universe. The universe does not occupy itself with pointless activities. It is simple and does not apply separate laws for living creatures, inanimate objects, humans, animals and other particulars. The status and significance of every piece is the same, just like a mother's love for all her children.

In fact, physicists think that even this many laws is too much for the universe and search for one all-encompassing law. While they seek out one combined law of physics, we will examine how the laws we already know of direct our lives. The other essential principle that we are aware of is that all the laws of the universe work together, so for every new circumstance that arises, there is more than one factor. In other words, there is more than one force behind every motion but one is always dominant. However, regardless of the significance of each event, the trigger is always simple. In actual fact, the trigger mechanism is always the simplest part of every system.

In terms of the universe, it is the process of squeezing that forms the trigger factor. This compression creates densification and due to the energy used, this densification causes an expansion in the mass of the unit volume. An increase in the energy within, as we previously pointed out, means an increase in mass. This phenomenon results from the universe's main equation: $E = MC2$. E= energy , M = mass , C = speed of light (constant). What we need to understand here is that the equilibrium of the equation contains a cosmic balance; when you increase the energy of any object, its mass also expands and when you expand the mass, its energy also increases.

Returning to the start of our discussion, if we surmise that, 'It, or something, was so compressed that eventually its inner reaction created the universe,' no physicist will object as this their very own discourse. Here we will not be debating which laws of physics belong to which scientist. That is not in our remit. We will also leave aside the matter of whether or not there was divine intervention. Another proposition that physicists will not object to is this: the main dynamic that began the universe will always be there as the dynamic that started, and will continue to start, everything. Therefore, the dynamic of beginning needs to be examined some more.

Firstly, if we want to start something new in our life, we must completely accept the need to create density by squeezing and compressing our life. We can't start anything without this process. The boundless universe only came about this way. If there had been an easier way, it would surely have found it, and if such a road does exist, it is unfortunately not in our universe. We have no choice but to live our lives in this bell jar and live by its rules. Our ancestors, who had an answer to everything, said, 'Cometh the hour, cometh the man.' Come what may, you will squeeze and be squeezed.

If there has there been a revolution, naturally there must have been a repressive regime before it. If a baby is to be born, the mother's stomach will swell so much, she will have difficulty moving. Are you inventing something? You need to work like a dog, squeezing your brain through a mangle. If despair and ambition swell you up until you are about to explode, you won't be able to explode, but will wait until the last moment. When the moment comes, take care not to attribute it to an apple falling from the tree or the mouldy cheese in the cultures cabinet. Just as God has no conductor's baton, so too does the universe not have its own special messengers. Unless you yourself make a cosmic gateway through your wall, it won't be possible for the apple to fall on the gate latch.

If you want to start your working life with a good job, you will be tormented by years of studying at the strictest schools, stressing over exams and grappling with the fear of failure. If you want to be wealthy, you must either work hard to qualify at a myriad of colleges, or approach it from another direction, dodging the law, doing whatever it takes and being prepared to endure years of prison if you get caught. You may want to be seen as a beautiful, good, clever and attractive woman, so you make a great investment in yourself in order to be liked, secretly striving to grab other's attention, but you can't possibly know how far this repression will go. The same is true for men who want to be perceived as handsome, rich, intelligent and attractive. This is the expansion of the mass that makes up your unit volume. But the mass that makes up the unit volume of each material is different and we sometimes start from different points to each other. That is down to your luck. The unit volumes of oxygen and mercury are extremely different and consequently their respective fates vary greatly.

Nothing in life can start without compression and tension - of that you can be sure. Never think that anything fresh and positive will open its wings and arrive of its own accord. If whatever may have been there 14 billion years ago had not become so compressed and dense, today's universe would never have been born. There is nothing for free and everything comes at a price. Everything requires its own outcome, like the two elements of a maths or physics equation. The essence of the universe is conformity and equilibrium. One side of an equation cannot be greater or lesser than the other.

In this context, there is no benefit from believing those who declare they have discovered esoteric secrets and attempt to hoodwink us with easy wins and false starts. We cannot reach fulfilment by writing our wishes on paper then putting them away in a drawer. No-one has ever become rich or experienced passionate love by making an inner wish and waiting for its effortless execution. This is a difficult endeavour, which must travel along the tracks of patience, never revealing which is your stop.

Firstly, we should be like the cosmos itself. Just like the cosmos, we should fill and empty, flow, compress, explode and scatter - just like wind, air and water. We should learn from all our cells to compress and loosen. We should tightly wrap our core like the electron cloud around the nucleus of an atom. We should grasp our desires with the strength of thousands of tons of nitroglycerine, like quarks clinging to each other.

BOREDOM

If to begin is to expend accumulated energy, then to succeed is to reach new glittering summits. The process of beginning and achieving success is mostly difficult and arduous. However much we doubt our chances of success, the physicists insist there is always a possibility, although it may be small. According to their theory, no particle can remain trapped inside a cell forever; in other words, there is no impregnable prison in the universe. (Of course, we are not talking about lazy particles - there are none of these in cosmic existence. Everything quivers and turns of its own volition.)

Recent physicists have a sympathetic side and however significant their findings are, they never shy away from giving them ordinary or even comical names. At the same time, the theory of relativity has even found its way into our everyday language. For quite a while now, black holes have been a much-discussed topic amongst the general public, and the same is true of other theories of the universe. Physicists must have renamed 'quantum leaps' as 'tunnelling' when science became popular with the general public. Its original name was enough of a joke, but why stop at one when you can have two?

Our previous understanding was that if a particle is trapped inside impenetrable walls with no exit (incarcerated for want of a better word), it cannot get out, but the truth is somewhat different. In this case, you might think that the famous Buddhist koan about a goose in a bottle was narrated especially for physicists. The story goes like this: the Zen master calls his student and tells him that he raised a gosling inside a narrow-necked bottle and that it had now grown and needed to be removed from it. He says that he wants him to find a way to set the goose free without harming the bottle or the goose. After weeks of contemplation, the young student has still not found an answer. One day, as he is sitting in his room engrossed in worries about this uncompleted homework, he suddenly leaps to his feet and runs towards his teacher's hut shouting, 'The goose is out! The goose is out!' The teacher doesn't ask how the goose got out.

There is also a goose in the atomic nucleus: the alpha particle. The area around this nucleus is wrapped with an electric cloud of such force that it cannot be punctured and breached. The alpha particle inside the atom attempts escape a billion times a second, but alas it is not possible to escape from the atom's carafe. But one day, maybe eight million years later, it will butt its head once more against the atom's carafe and suddenly find itself outside. This might seem to you like an incredibly long and exhausting endeavour. (When we look at the life of subatomic particles, while life expectancy is sometimes very short - for example, the life of a pi-meson is one in a 100 millionth of a second - sometimes it is long enough to be considered be eternal life, just like the life of a proton, which is 10^{32} years (a trillion times a trillion times a billion years). As such a duration of time has not yet passed in the universe and neither has a disintegrated proton been found, perhaps we should refer to its life span as eternal.)

In summary, no numeric figure is a stranger to the universe - from the youngest to the oldest - and no wall of the universe is impregnable. This does not imply that the walls are faulty, but rather that there is a universal lottery and at the end of an unknown time period, there could be great rewards. Fantastical stories are the real stories of the universe, and fantasy is their original creative art form, which illustrates that every bottleneck has an outlet, every problem will be resolved in time, every prison can be escaped and the most improbable can come about if desired and striven for (including dreams, wishes and the relevant willpower). In other words, there is no place for hopelessness in the universe, but patience and persistence must be fearlessly deployed.

The magician hides Rapunzel in a tower with no stairs or doors, but is unable to prevent her running off to the palace to marry. The Rapunzel phenomenon is a perfect quantum leap. So many people who say they are imprisoned inside their marriage until death releases them, suddenly find they are free. What is it that happens? Anything is possible. One day your partner comes to you and asks to talk. You sit down. For a while, your lover's eyes are fixed on the ground. Then, as if emptying out all the breathe inside in one rush, the inconceivable words spill out in front of you,

'I love someone else. Maybe I don't deserve it, but I am asking for your understanding.'

Or perhaps those words will suddenly spill from your mouth one day when you can no longer endure your partner's jealousy, petulance and endless questioning about your relationships with work colleagues.

'That's it! Let's just get divorced and put an end to this torture...'

First of all, your ears can't believe what has come out of your mouth. How did you manage to say it? Where did you find the courage? Now there is no turning back. Inside, you feel lighter already. The genie is out of the lamp and the prevarications suddenly disappear out of your way - your children's educational plans, mortgage payments for the new house, what will your partner-friends-relatives say, how you will stand up to the relationship counsellors. You see a huge universe at your feet and the second sentence slowly departs from you lips as if you are taking your maiden step.

'I'm going...'

It wasn't planned at all. It had been building up had a for years, as the spring of life reset itself after every friction, until finally it released, letting the goose out of the bottle. Just like all the children who bear the torment of being labelled as inept, wear the yolk of 'under achievement' round their necks and feel that every road is closed to them. How many of them late go on to be initiators and leaders heading in new directions. You have given up on your wayward daughter who is never at home and settle for simply hoping that she does not get into serious trouble; but years later she is settled and happily married. The quiet girl in the class, who is barely noticed and doesn't even make the grade for university, years later grasps the bar of relativity to emerge from the pack of third-rate civil servants as the next Einstein.

Just like the alpha particles, life too is continually digging tunnels from one space to another, particularly in the places you think are impassable. Sometimes it takes a long time, but those who know to wait and never throw out the pickaxe will have their reward. I wonder if there is any prison that has had no escapees? Yet for thousands of years we have been striving to build jails with no way out. All prisons can be exited without completing the full sentence. Even the highest micro-security measures cannot make it impossible to get out. A magnitude nine earthquake can bring down all our systems. Or if you can't get out alive, your lifeless body leaves.

Wouldn't the Dalton brothers always have found a way to escape their cell? If a product you have introduced to the world has a universal appeal, no-one can stand in its way. Despite the many heroic cartoon characters to emerge in the media, only some manage to supersede all cultural differences and take hold across the globe. One of these is the Daltons, because they escape from every prison. Their forte is digging tunnels and this has a universal appeal. Even genies trapped for eternity eventually find salvation. Wasn't the genie in Aladdin's lamp the same? Even if you sent it to the furthest end of the universe inside a stone, it will still find a springboard to get out. It maybe 10 million years later, but it would still find it, because we are leapers. Our building blocks are leapers...because time itself leaps. Indeed, everything leaps.

As you can see, in life nothing is impossible. The thickest walls can be breached, the furthest distances can be travelled, and all without making any actual physical changes. All you have to do is leap, and to allow this to happen, you just need to wait ready by the wall and knock. How many people have not at some point in their life felt as if a truculent teacher is determined not to give them a pass mark? Yet one day, suddenly the magical pass mark appears at the top of their exam paper. All you do is unswervingly fix on your desire to pass the exam - just like the alpha particle hitting its head against the energy shield of the nucleus - using all the neurons in your brain to knock against the shield and, with all the energy of your spirit, pressurise the jar in which you are trapped, bearing the pain of despair but never losing hope as you remain resolute inside the same meaningless cycle. Don't forget that every door on which you knock can open. Just keep on stubbornly knocking.

If you like, we can go back to school again. Wasn't it podgy Ahmed, who could barely hold a knife and fork, that tried to pick up the prettiest girl in the class? Wasn't he terrible at lessons too? Wasn't it Süheyla, that the boys in the class barely even noticed, that became one of the most famous models ten years later? That is in fact the main rule of marketing and haggling. A good marketeer is an indomitable warrior - an alpha particle that hits its head against the wall until it opens, never getting bored and never entertaining regret. The Romany people have a strong, marketing instinct, and just like the alpha particles inside them, they harness their energy to travel the roads, never tiring or losing interest until they have sold all their wares. Their spirit and consciousness is constantly in conversation with the deep world inside their bodies; there is an area like clear water between their cells and consciousness, which is unsullied by social bric-a-brac.

Years ago, I had started commuted home via a different route and always saw a Romany girl selling flowers by the traffic lights at the last corner before home. She always took her place by the traffic lights at the same time, and when they changed to red, she would entreat me to buy a flower with sweet cajolery. For as long as I can remember, I have never had any interest in flowers. I only ever grew edible plants in my garden. While the neighbours garden was carpeted in grass and adorned with multicoloured flowers, mine was full of tomatoes, peppers, cucumbers and corn plants. So, naturally, I didn't buy any flowers from her, but she never stopped trying to persuade me. She carried on for months, every time with the same insistence as the first. I developed a relationship of sorts with her: a relationship in which our energies were knitted together - hers in selling and mine in not buying. She was ever adamant, because her genetic heritage signalled that with every attempt she was getting closer. But I was adamant too, and determined not to buy. This stand-off continued for four months. During this time, every time she saw me at the lights she would run over to try again. She used every trick. Then she disappeared and I didn't see her for about a week.

On the eighth day, she was back again. As I waited at the lights, I saw her roaming in her own world with the flowers in her hands. When she neared the car, she suddenly recognised me, crying 'Brother!' and began to run towards me. This time she might make a sale, but even if she didn't, she would carry on trying until the end. We were living in the same universe, in which she could sell me flowers even if I didn't want them. The Romany people know about impossibility, but also the billion to one probability it contains inside it. That's why there is no retreat until they achieve their goal, right until the end, and this is what makes them indomitable warriors. They don't get offended, they don't tire and they don't get bored - atomic nuclei reflected into our world. When she got to the car, she was out of breath and angrily threw the flower through my open window. She shouted emphatically,
'If you are going to buy one, buy one now!'

The flower had fallen on the lap of the female friend sitting next to me. If there had been a man sitting next to me, I would have picked it up from the floor and handed it back, but I didn't have the courage to take a flower from the lap of a woman and throw it away. The flower was sold and the alpha particle leapt from the nucleus into another space.

Everything in existence, which is in itself the universe, has the same consciousness of unconditional progression, patience and endurance. We never stop, just like the universe, which has been expanding and spreading for 14 billion years. When you think about it, how many of us actually stop when our desires come to fruition. Who says that the money they earn is enough? Is there a child that backs off, taking pity on their poor parents as they strive to give them all they want? To be ceaselessly directed towards the new is written into our building blocks, just as it was written on the first day, which sentenced us to continually seek out the new - the whole universe...

And the moral of the story is that the universe does not like impossibility and neither do we. When our arms are not strong enough, our imagination takes hold of our dreams. 'One day, definitely...' is a belief we prize. The impossible is not a concept connected to the universe. Here, everything leaps, runs, changes place and changes shape. Every day a new fire burns, and in time periods we think of as short, trillions of sparks are scattered, starting new lives and finishing others. In the universe, every process is a life. The life of creatures, inanimate objects, events, concepts, emotions, as it keeps recreating itself and taking on new forms. Every wish is the spell that concocts the new. Look around you, and you will see the many things that we once thought of as impossible.

When time began to swell the cosmic core, the moment created space, allowing the cosmic core to don three dimensions and grow.

Afterwards, the 'moment' blessed the process forming inside it, christening it life and giving meaning to all the dimensions. As it progressed, leaving behind tracks with every new step, time came into existence as the universe's memory.

TRACKS

In order to continue its existence, the cosmos needed to remember. When creating the new, the universe references the old, turning itself into an endless string. This is why the tracks must be recognised and the previous steps copied. It is only able to exist by repeating itself. If it was to lose its past, it would lose itself, because all existence has been founded upon its past. The old adage, 'The future depends on what we do today,' contains the core intrinsic belief that what has gone before will shape the future. Perhaps the reason this belief is shared by all of us is because it has a universal origin. The signposts of history illuminate our future and this is the reflection of a universal ordering of our lives, because whatever exists today will exist in the future, even if in a changed form.

The tracks of your experiences cannot be carried inside you and you cannot drive them. Work done without serving an apprenticeship is unsuccessful for that reason. Enduring buildings can only be constructed step by step. The man we spent a passionate night with after a chance meeting in a bar, cinema, beach, bus or similar random venue, or the woman we rushed into marriage with, can only lead us into an unstable relationship. The cosmos expands by constantly mimicking its own birth. This is its growing up process and at every new beginning it adds another detail. Scientists call this mutation.

We too start off as a cell when taking our first steps towards the life prepared for us, just like the cosmic birth known as the Big Bang. We follow the same path and process: separating, combining and multiplying, just like cosmic expansion, the cell splits trillions of times to carve its existence. Throughout this process, we all have a map in our hands, a map that is etched by the life journey of our history over trillions of years. The map drawn by DNA, and known as genome, never leaves our side. We carry it with us everywhere, from cradle to grave. It is our most important inheritance and we have arrived at today after billions of years of following this trail. Does this seem surprising to you? It's extraordinary isn't it? In actual fact, it's very simple. The Great Genome book says:

'Follow your trail!' That's all...

The spell is hidden in your trail. The spirit of time is hidden there, showing us the way like an angel perched on our shoulders. When we arrive in the world, the structure of the hollow cortex in our head is all the same. Our consciousness forms by reflecting the world around us. This is how we perceive our world and, as far as we can see, the universe as well. Our brain's perception is visual. Our feelings operate in the limbic system under the cortex. Our brain cannot perceive the depth of matter and

.

it is not possible to feel the secret of genesis in the cortex. Unfortunately, a knowledge-gate opening on to the secret of universal existence has not yet formed in the cortex. Maybe eventually we will create it ourselves and in one million years' time an eye to the universe will open up within the cortex. Perhaps this is what Buddhists respectfully refer to as the third eye. But for now, we only live the life we see in our mirror. We want wealth and prosperity and we want it immediately, whereas everything is achieved step by step. The distinction between our desire and the clothes we see in the shop window or the car we see in the showroom has still not formed in our sensory centre.

Why do young girls bemoan the fact that a prince does not come and whisk them away to a new life? Why do others always win the hand of the king's daughter while our son doesn't get a look in? Undoubtedly, no-one would want to share the same torment as the silken-haired Rapunzel, who was enslaved by a witch from birth, before being imprisoned in a tower when she reached 12 and later forced to wander in the wilderness. No-one is interested in how Rapunzel kept warm in the tower when the winter snow fell, or what she ate and drank when she was cast into the wilderness. We ignore the fact that Rapunzel's desire for the prince and her subsequent ordeal are the most significant factors in completing the fairy tale tableau.

Similarly, we overlook the fact that Cinderella had to sweep the floor and do the laundry from dawn until dusk before climbing into her bed amongst the household rubbish. We don't think of how cold and painful her hands must have been when she held them over the lukewarm coals of an extinguished fire. It is only the happy endings that draw our attention. It's as if we fast forward through all the pain and suffering to arrive quickly at the end. But life is not just endings - it matures and grows step by step.

Are these thousands of arduous steps enough? Sadly, you cannot play an instrument the minute you have paid for it. Neither do we know how much more you will have to pay. We must wait, but most of the time our lifespan is not adequate. Therefore, we need to scatter the seeds as we walk. After that, it is down to the seed and the universe - not us. Perhaps this is what we don't understand. Scatter thousands of seeds and out of these thousands, three will grow into trees, two will bear fruit and one will provide dense shade. Don't get bored and don't restrict your life to these seeds. It is only after you throw them that they become individual seeds and cease to belong to you. Our successes and the prosperity and wealth that we gain are also not ours. They exist of their own accord and with their own inner dynamics. We can only rest for a while in their shade.

The lottery is considered to be won effortlessly by chance, but the desire to get rich quick through playing the lottery is created by the misplaced logic of humankind. How many people who become rich from a huge windfall actually stay rich? We may think that there is not much meaning in the expression 'Easy come, easy go'. However, that is not the case. Without a trail to follow, nothing can survive into the future. There is just one reason why humans and all other creatures have progressed for millions of years without getting lost and that is because there is a trail. The trail engraves existence into the entity of the universe. The trail is patience and tireless repetitions.

The probability of falling at the first step is always high. In the universe as a whole, more than a trillion times a trillion times a trillion such steps have been made. The chance of falling at the second step is lower, and then lower still by the time you get to the tenth step. By the time you arrive at the thousandth step, you have a much better chance of a solid future than before. The moral of the story is that any wealth that arrives at the first step has a high probability of being frittered away.

The universe harnesses all its forces to destroy every new beginning. This is a cosmic trial or we could call it a cosmic weeding process. Our scientists have examined this principle more closely and given it the name 'natural selection'. Can we possibly believe that this principal, which applies to the life of all living creatures, is not valid for their possessions, companies and relationships? If we say that the building blocks of life, one of the greatest discoveries of the universe, and the processes that flow through them are not applicable to commonplace issues, aren't we negating the totality of universal existence? Bearing that in mind, what might happen to the wealth that arrives at the first step from something like the lottery? The whole world and his wife will come to you for help. Sometimes the requests will be more than the money you have. Cousins you haven't spoken to for years will arrive out of the blue. A multitude of needy people will seek you out to request a share of your divine gift. You will be showered in curses if you don't reciprocate. Local mafia will be at your door offering to protect you for a fee, and eventually you will be forced to choose protection from one of the competing gangs that have knocked at your door. All the random things you have ever wanted to do, but never managed will be swimming around in your head. Charities will ask you for meeting after meeting. Your partner and children will present their wish list in the most imploring tones. Thieves will have your house under observation and fleece you at the first opportunity.

You may not welcome any of this, but that is the outcome of that which is attained at the first step. Does wealth accumulated over several centuries induce the same problems? Well, of course! But these problems dissipate at the first breeze, just like dust particles on steel, because the tracks of history are the greatest guarantor of the future. In that case, perhaps we can subscribe to the following definition: the universe expends all its force on scattering the first object it receives, but bounty obtained as a result of a long and arduous process can only be dislodged by another arduous process. However great the immediate pleasures of rapid gains might be, it is still not wise to take the easy way out. There is a typical, somewhat stereotype example that can be used to illustrate - Meltem's rapid rise and fall in the office.

As a graduate of the type of university where education is in a foreign language and the fees are make it only accessible to the children of the rich, Meltem made quite a splash when she arrived. In reality, she was a talentless person, who knew how to use her sex appeal to make up for her negligible abilities. She rapidly became promoted to a managerial position, overtaking colleagues who had regularly sweated blood for their career and knew the job inside out. Eventually, the resentment of her colleagues built up to such a point that they were forced to tell her that the promotion was nothing to do with her ability and that the position was rightfully theirs. However, the deed was done and she was now their manager.

But Meltem's pot had not yet completely boiled - in fact, it wasn't even lukewarm yet. Brewing is a torturous, laborious process; the coffee sits inside the water as it heats up, waiting patiently for its essence to slowly permeate the surrounding liquid. To brew is to quietly but meticulously undergo a process that requires both heat and patience. Meanwhile, the universe never forgets to sift through its contents. Over 90% of that which is gained at the first step goes straight into the bin. Life has a multitude of ways to carry out its sifting process. Sperms are sifted at every step of their progress. In order to reach the egg, they need to pass through countless acid pools and only one out of the millions makes it into the egg. Fish scatter millions of eggs into the far reaches of the sea, but only a miniscule fraction of these is able to transform into a fish. Enduring achievements are always attained at the end of a gruelling process. Successfully learning how to speak, read and write, understand maths, physics, chemistry, economics, politics, drawing or even playing a musical instrument all come at the end of a long journey down many roads. The same is true of building skyscrapers; every durable object and concept trails a long track from the past.

In life, if you have no tracks, you have no future. A long track indicates a long future and conversely a short track indicates a short future. Meltem was sifted out during the company's first redundancy programme. Years later, I saw her at the door of another company that I was visiting on business, and she told me she come to drop off her CV as she was jobhunting. She was still a good-looking woman, but her eyes now had dark shadows around them. Deep down I felt as if some waves had just struck a wall and were rebounding back again. As she scurried off, I looked back at her, but she had turned the corner and disappeared. Meltem was never one for perseverance, endurance and learning. Yet without any of these, she had dipped a toe into the flow of achievement. She had some success, but the problem was that she was not able to hold onto it. The same applied to her marriages.

Life's lottery has another dynamic apart from its characteristic of being an easy gain. The lottery also represents an energy that was not personally created by us. Looked at in this light, the gains of Meltem and those like her are at great risk of being sifted out by life's huge dredger. In fact, these two lottery characteristics complement each other, just like two sides of a coin. The lottery is a concept that so perfectly fits the 'uncertainty principle' expounded by Werner Heisenberg in 1927 that to say that it incorporates the same dynamics will hopefully not put us on a par with the postmodern knowledge marketeers that give everything a quantum name. The uncertainty principle permits the particles to loan energy, limited by a specific period of time. During this process, energy is used by the particle before it is separated again. In this way, a particle can leave a steel tin it is enclosed, but the energy that pushed it outside is soon forced away from the particle.

Banking systems also work according to this law of physics. Isn't it obvious that any profession that doesn't apply natural laws to its operations will not succeed in continuously growing and developing? In all likelihood, the banking and finance system's global embrace and ability to continuously develop comes from its adherence to cosmic laws. The system works by sometime later taking back whatever it gives and as we all know, loaned money does not makes us rich. We shouldn't forget that natural laws do not tender out their usage rights to any professional grouping, but those professions and businesses that are founded on their principles withstand the test of time. It is for this reason that the financial market, whose core purpose is to loan and then take back, has become one of the building blocks of our economic life.

Borrowing and the lottery jackpot both share the common value of not being attained as a result of a long endeavour. Borrowing is the transfer of someone else's money into your orbit - just like energy, which is its equivalent in cosmic life. But it's only temporary, and the duration varies according to the nature of the transfer. In quantum mechanics, being able to skip into another space with borrowed energy is called tunnelling. In our example, the space jumped to is a higher quality of life, or new possibilities provided by finance. Whether it is establishing a new business, modernising the premises or paying off a debt, in essence it means stepping onto another platform that could not be reached with your previous energy level. You can repay your borrowed energy in one lump sum or by instalments and the length of the payback period is always different.

So what kind of things can we borrow? Everything...because the universe has everything. Bearing in mind that in our closed universe, the source of everything is a core going back 14 billion years, and that nothing from outside could enter its expanding body, everything that exists today, both material and spiritual, is this core itself and contains the same energy structure. Consequently, if there is such a process as borrowing, then it is unconceivable to think of it not existing. We are probably even in an energy-borrowing relationship with the life energy that brought us into being, and the reason why every living creature must die is hidden inside this cosmic law. There is no cure for death, because life is based on borrowed energy.

As we swim in the cosmic sea, the spillage seeping into our perceptions through the cracks tentatively reflects this information into our mind through a screen of illusions. We find this in some fables, anonymous myths or in the tales of storytellers, who are generally more perceptive than others. Most of these tales, which we instinctively want our children to read despite turning our backs on them as adults, are actually individual reflections of the borrowing of cosmic energy. As midnight strikes, Cinderella's gilt carriage turns into a pumpkin, the coachman turns into a rat and her elegant lace dress is reduced to rags; this is a reflection of borrowed energy from the quantum world being given back after a set period. King Midas is granted his wish that everything he touches turns to gold, but after a while, with the permission of the god Dionysus, he disposes of this power by washing in the Paktalos River.

If we return once more to lottery gains, we firstly need to reaffirm our belief in money as a force. The fact that money has the power to single-handedly buy (transfer) objects and create values shows that it is indeed a force. Here we see this force being transferred to a person through the medium of the lottery. We cannot say that money is virtual and outside the laws of physics; it can be converted into material objects when desired, therefore showing it is one of the carriers of force in the universe. To bring this about, billions of human arms and brains work machines and the created value is shared out to be used. Looked at from the angle of the universe's structure, filling a battery with energy or filling a wallet with money are similar processes and come about through similar laws. With the smallest effort, you can find numerous examples of the fact that everything that might happen to the money in your wallet or cash till, is also relevant to the energy stored in your batteries.

The process of borrowing/lending is the transfer of money that has not been earned by expending energy. Just as you can obtain this through the rules of the finance system, with the correct energy transmission it can be achieved at the right time in the right place of the universal flow. Perhaps the sensitive balance and system can be explained by the concept of 'chance'. Whether it is called chance or something else, at its foundation is the system of cosmic energy borrowing. Gravitational force carries massless particles called gluons and if there are no gluons, there is no gravity. The values we have formed around our economic life are carried by the thing we call money. Gluons and money enable the transfer of both forces - perhaps money is not just a carrier of force but also a force in itself.

Following this logic, if we see the dynamic of wealth transferred by the lottery as a temporary energy transfer, we need to enter into a harmonious flow with it rather than resist the system. As this energy will leave us at the end of an unknown period, the best approach must be to assist the movement of this energy. It might be beneficial to the movement of energy to immediately go out and buy something with our new financial resources; or you might prefer to take into consideration that it comes from a societal source and set up a system for sending it back. A clever way to do this might be some kind of foundation. In this way, you can avoid the build-up and constriction of energy that leads to its sudden dissipation in an explosion.

Is it mere coincidence that those who have gained huge wealth set up various foundations with significant sums of their fortune, as if they are all in agreement with each other? Or is it the result of a delicate and deep sentiment connected to the flows of the cosmic world? We should not forget that the basis of a significant amount of wealth is a kind of universal lottery. No matter how clever you are and how hard you work, the most you will achieve in 15-20 years will be a house to live in and a car to sweep you off your feet. Anything more is the surplus value accumulated from the economic activities of others. That being the case, what is written here need not concern most of us.

What has been explained is true in individual life, but could it have a different meaning in a societal dimension? Is it possible? As there is only one universe, I am sure its rules are valid everywhere. Let's take a look at economic theories. Isn't the main reason for economic crises insufficient spending? Don't economics books and economic theories state that absolute saving is a mortal enemy of the economy? (As accumulating money in a bank account enables the bank to transfer money to others in credit, it does not enter the realm of societal saving.)

What happens when the accumulation grows more than required? Money and the associated accumulated value, in other words the flow of energy, is insufficient. The value builds up squashed inside a repository. From an economic point of view, when there is no spending, other economic units receive insufficient income and are left without energy. When they have no income, they cannot pursue their own activities and they too completely cease to spend. At some later point, the economic units that are bereft of income grind to a halt. This means an interruption in the supply of income (energy). When supply falls, prices rise (inflation). As a result, bread costs the same sum of money that would previously have bought a car and society becomes completely impoverished. Complete impoverishment is the explosion and scattering of accumulated value, leaving nothing behind. Our storage units have exploded and the compacted energy has been returned to the universe. In the language of the universe, the escape of compressed energy to mix with other particles is the equivalent to a rich person or society becoming impoverished in this way. If this discourse belonged to economists its credibility rating would rise, but the secrets of the universe are taken less seriously when explained by a Buddhist priest or shaman.

However, is it a coincidence that all religions preach generosity? Or are they trying to protect us from what will happen if we do not live in accordance with the rules of existence? The rich giving aid to the poor is something beyond what is known as kindness and holy altruism, which has no meaning from the point of view of universal values. Religious rules are in fact a sign of the fact that in our relationships we have not stepped outside of cosmic laws and dynamics. If we extract ourselves from the pressures and stresses of everyday life to look into life more deeply, it is not such a difficult thing, and we see the secret messages in its tremors. For example, Zen Buddhism is not a religion, but the concepts it reveals are not that different from those embodied by the sacred religious texts.

All discourses shaped in the depths of existence quantify the accumulation of wealth and related greed as a wrong deed which should be eschewed. Whether or not this proposition is correct, we cling as closely to the force known as wealth as a heroin addict does to his drug. Why is that we cling on? Readers must give their own answer, or explain it as a fault or incorrect adjustment in the limbic system of life and pass over it. Whichever way we look at it, what can be done? Are we trying to hoodwink the universe by setting up foundations with our surplus wealth, or is it that we will find a different and healthy trail for our life this way? Are we capable of being individuals who do not feel the need to borrow, do not complain about paying back our debts and have absorbed the necessity of this into our consciousness. Can we strangle our greed? Before we move onto this subject, we need to better clarify the other dynamics of the evolution of all our relationships and the framework of our dynamics.

CONSTRICTION

If one edge of cosmic existence is constricted, the other edge expands. We now know that the beginning made its journey without any constriction, but is every beginning good? Should we constrict everything? The universe is expanding every day and the speed of expansion is constant everywhere. Where might we be taken by gathering together and proliferating under these conditions - in other words constriction? 'Give me a break! I'll explode,' is a warning that contains innate truth. What does it mean when people say, 'You've gone too far'? What are we trying to say with the words, 'That's it.'

On the other hand, when we first become teenagers, don't we learn off by heart the most important factor of the fine art of chasing the opposite sex? Isn't the rule, 'Don't pressurise the female so much that she will clam up and don't be to annoying? If you don't get it right, you might incur reactions like:
'Pull yourself together'
'Where is all this coming from?'
'Don't you have anything better to do!'
'Now you're bugging me...'

We used to have a second principle: the one that runs away gets chased. Allow freedom of movement. Show the spaces that allow for freedom and facilitate passage there. The road on which you are escaping is the road to freedom that you showed, and she will follow behind you without even noticing. Come what may, if you want someone to take a positive step towards you, you need to take a step back and avoid pushing too hard. In short, we don't like being constricted and err more on the side of expansion. In fact, all living creatures are like that. When we are put under pressure, we feel the need to react, even becoming aggressive. Dogs react like that, snakes react like that...

Living creatures are like that, but are inanimate objects the same? As our core is founded on the material world we call inanimate, these reactions are shared by everyone and everything. Not one of us is won over by being pressurised. Depending on the person, some of us give an immediate reaction, some wait and react later on. All living creatures are the same. Elements we call inanimate demonstrate different reactions to being under pressure. Those made up of gas have a high tolerance, but solid elements give an immediate reaction to being constricted. Pressurised objects start to vibrate at particle level, which makes them heat up. If they are squeezed even more, they turn into a hot lava. Because of this pressure, the centre of the earth is a molten mass in which all the elements are melted.

Our earth was never a fireball and therefore it is not the case that its exterior cools down and the interior stays hot. When the heat, which built doe to the mass created by gravitational pressure in the centre, turned into a cauldron that boiled the area, the centre consequently formed of melted lava. As long as the earth stays in its place, the boiling lava stays in place, but sometimes it is ejected into daylight through volcanoes. We live upon a mass that has densified from being compressed towards the centre by gravity. The same gravity pushes us down towards the ground. That is why our graves are in the ground. The God of Death is deep down, somewhere in the land of darkness.

Just as we do not like to be pressured, we also do not like to be shut in, especially if the place where we are enclosed is restrictive. We want our home to be wide and open at the front, so that we can see the horizon from the doorway, watch the sun rise through our windows or wave goodbye to it from our balcony. Isn't incarceration the greatest punishment? Although the prison may be warm and fill our stomachs, the mere thought of being stuck there is enough to terrify us. We refer to relationships we are fed up with as 'like being in prison'.

The meaning of freedom, one of the most valued facets of life, is to be unconstricted - in every sense. As well as being constricted in a place, every other kind of constriction damages our freedom and consequently our soul. From the very first day, freedom has been the home of our spirit. In fact, freedom is our spirit itself and one cannot live without the other. After it had been scattered far and wide by the Big Bang, our existence discovered something new; this was its new form and its name was freedom. When freedom is used, it preserves its meaning, leaping over all the obstacles before us to advance. The hormonal balance of the metabolism reflects this structure and when we can exist freely, our primal brain, known as the limbic system, releases hormones filling us with feelings of happiness and satisfaction. This is how we know ourselves. Our cosmic core communicates with us via our hormonal balance. The genie of the lamp also waits hopefully to escape for thousands of years. Its escape creates such great happiness that he places himself at the full disposal of Aladdin, who after all had only wiped the dust from the lamp.

Similarly, space travel was the dream of our race for thousands of years. Although we have everything here and are comfortable, we cherish the idea of being able to travel to the stars. To journey is to be unconfined. It is the image, reflected in our lives, of the character and secret code written into our core by the universe's first day. To journey is to be an integral part of the whole movement that started completely together with us. Besides, in life how many situations are there that exasperate us more than incarceration? This is true not just for humans, but for all living creatures... How many animals enjoy lazing about in a cage? No matter how well the animal's stomach is filled by another, it longs to escape to another place, regardless of how hungry it might end up being.

Subatomic particles are the same. They react to being closed in just like us. For example, when you close an electron into a cell from which it cannot escape, and restrict the volume of the cell, the electron starts to move more quickly. As the pressure increases, the electron becomes more frenzied, bashing its head against the walls. Of course, even though we can't hear it screaming, 'Let me out', we can imagine what it's going through. When we constrict an element or molecule, the result is similar, and the atoms break into powerful tremors. The kinetic energy produced as a result of the tremors turns to heat, while the atoms, which are broken down by the vibrations, slide over one another taking on a liquid form - just like the molten lava created from iron at the earth's core.

In short, the whole universe, including the human race, does not like being pressured and closed in. Just as too much pressure changes the physical structure of matter, it also affects our character, revealing very different traits hidden beneath our identity. The liquifying and effusion of iron, one of the world's hardest materials, is a small example of this. The chief proponent is not heat but pressure, as we touched upon above, or looked at from another angle, energy. Extreme pressure must therefore mean mass coming head on with intense, powerful energy. The force of the pressure passes to the atom, which starts to tremor with this energy and heat, and the kinetic result of this vibration is activated. As a consequence, the atoms' bonds loosen and spread outwards.

That being the case, isn't it unfair to expect humans under pressure to do what iron, platinum and titanium themselves cannot do? In the face of pressure, everyone unravels, although to different degrees. Just as the melting points of copper and titanium are very different, even the melting point of the same metal will vary if other materials are present within it. Therefore, the degree and timing of our reactions will each be different. As we said before, pressure changes our behaviour, exposing previously unknown sides to our character.

To be able to withstand stress, is a state revered by our culture. Interrogators know these resilient people well, people who can absorb the energy coming at them for a long time without changing their form of existence. It is difficult to elicit information from them, but not impossible. Every molecular bond has a splitting temperature. Some of us unravel immediately when we first meet energy, just like the sudden evaporation of alcohol, and release what is pent up inside us. Others , like water, are more resistant and wait a while before evaporating. In the terminology of interrogation, releasing your secret inner information is called squealing, although the experts use another term – breaking down.

Under pressure, we reveal the information we were not supposed to give. Interrogation techniques are nothing but the employment of pressure and force. You must be wondering what exactly is employed? It might be physical force, beating or electrocution. In other cases, force is applied over a period of time, such as water dripping on the head or keeping a person in extremely bright light for hours or even days. (The applied energy is expected to yield better results by getting the subject to resonate and this is another technical subject.) Women also know how to extract secret information from men as part of their genetic heritage. A woman's instinct tells her just how much, how long and in what way to pressurise the man. It is for this reason that men confess to having affairs more often than women.

The result of pressure is not just the breakdown of resistance and the expulsion of the information you had hidden inside. It also causes you to move outside of the behaviour you have been taught. People who cheat when they are under intense pressure from their husband or wife are so numerous that no-one should be called to account for it. It is also common to see a family head who is unable to support the household or share the load with anyone else get up and go one day. No-one should be blamed for fleeing pressure.

When I first caught sight of Suleyman as I was on the way to work one morning, he seemed to be waiting for a friend in the park. By his side was a rucksack and a large plastic carrier bag full of unknown items. Over the following days, I saw him again at the same time on the same bench. His stance and clothing were not those of someone living on the streets. His neat, trimmed ginger beard, waistcoat, jacket and sports shoes indicated good taste. When I saw him at midday rummaging through the rubbish bin, I naively thought that he had dropped something in by accident. But then he started to eat the half-sandwich he had extricated from it. When I passed by one morning a few days later, I pressed 10 lira into his hand and then continued on my way. In my head, I was still incredulous that he was living on the streets and expected him to take offence at my giving him money. He was certainly surprised. I turned away without uttering a word and began to move off, but stopped when I heard him say,

'Sir...'He looked down and said, 'Thank you, you have made me ashamed.'

We were both awkward.

'Have a nice breakfast,' I said and walked on.

In the days after this, I sometimes gave him money and sometimes I stood and chatted to him. He spoke very well and it turned out he had studied abroad. His father was a manual worker in Belgium, and when he had nearly finished high school, he reached the point when he could no longer bear his father's pressure and beating, so he returned to Turkey. He said that he had been living on the streets since that day. In the end, his melted spirit had slipped out of the door into the street. Over the years, as he slowly cooled down, he had solidified among the street stones. He had been sleeping in his sleeping bag in parks for almost five years. He asked me for books to read. When he finished one, I would bring him another. He preferred the thick books as he finished the short ones too quickly. Thanks to my efforts, one corner of his bag turned into a library.

One summer day he asked me to bring him an old long-sleeved shirt of mine. When I asked the reason, he showed me his arms. Both his arms were covered in the scars of knife wounds. During the time when his father was beating him, he would slash himself out of anger, but now he was ashamed of people seeing his arms. One day, he had been just like the rest of us, enjoying life with a girlfriend who worked at a jewellers.

If young teenagers experience conflicting values in their family, school and friend circles and are at the same time are under heavy disciplinary pressure, they will in all likelihood lose their bearings. Under too much pressure, they exude inside other structures where they solidify - just as Suleyman was driven onto the streets. All of us have a different melting point and flow into different vessels. Unable to bear the pressure, Suleyman coalesced between the street stones. It is no secret that behind every person that flees from home is a chronic pressure. Nobody sleeps on the streets, shivering with cold, just for pleasure. But it is not every type of pressure that sends us into the streets. The pressure must be systematic and continue for a while in order to yield results. If you apply pressure, you must be ready for the results, because at the end of it, you will be faced with someone completely different. You need to have your new mold ready, because if not, your solution will flow into the first thing it finds and adopt its new form there. The mold can be called lifestyle, value system, expectations or goals.

Consequently, the lives of children and young people need to be considered as a whole during the shaping operation which is otherwise known as education, never losing sight of the fact that melted substances will flow into a ready vessel. It's not enough to simply send the child to the best school - you must maintain the discipline and goals of school in the home. But even that in itself is not enough; the same approach to life has to be adopted in everything, from the TV programmes your child watches, to their friendships and the type of computer games they play. Surely you don't think it's easy to melt a piece of metal? You need to know just how much to heat it up - in other words - the degree of pressure. First of all, you must have a vessel fit for purpose that will not melt along with the metal. You must keep in mind the danger of fire if you spill it randomly and that it will take shape from the place where it is spilt.

If you leave any gaps, or your hand trembles, the molten material will slip away and its new form will be created by its new location. If the open gap leads to a few undesirable friends, in a short while, you could end up with a very well-educated and sophisticated heroin addict or a prostitute who wonders from party to party looking for trade. Playing with energy is dangerous. Force can result in forming and molding, but to an equal degree, it also has the power to trash and burn. When working with electricity, we give our utmost attention and take every precaution. When operating a 100 ton press, we vigilantly steer scores of mechanisms. Therefore, when applying pressure to a person, we must exercise the same diligence if we want to avoid losing someone we care about.

Education, military training and family life all apply heavy pressure. The behavioural approaches to business that make the difference between success and failure require pressure. It's not possible to force behaviour to conform to societal norms by applying kindness and guidance that is more like the soft touch of a downy bird feather. The child whose every wish is granted will not grow to be the adult you envisaged, with civilised values and a healthy career. You cannot give shape to anything without applying some pressure. In fact, even a picture cannot be painted without the pressure of the brush, nor a book be written without the pressure of pen on paper.

If you are going to steer life, you must not take your hand from the wheel. Just as when you are driving a car, you must always keep in mind the heavy consequences of neglect. Every life hurtles down its road without stopping, just like a driverless car, and only disciplined, vigilant behaviour can prevent you, the person concerned and others being damaged by it. But even that is no guarantee; the cosmic structure weighs up its datasets and taps through millions of unknown equations before laying them out before us, taking no notice of the way we are behaving in the background. Undoubtedly, this is why life is ever full of surprises.

REMEMBERING

Just as it is not possible to double-guess what lays ahead in the world of atomic particles (Werner Heisenberg's Uncertainty Principle), the trillions of data that steer the balance and interactions of our whole life most of the time catch us unaware. But we should not despair too much. All of this should not stop us saying that we love someone. Calculate which stone you will roll, in which direction and at which speed, then throw the stone and leave the rest to life's own mechanism. If there is anything we have learnt since the birth of the universe, it is that even if the stone goes in the right direction but is wide of its target, the end result will in all probability still satisfy us.

The important thing for us is not to know everything, but to capture the rhythm of the universe and the flow of life. We have to decide how much poisonous mushroom to add to the wizard's cauldron. Nothing is simply either good or bad. The important thing is to understand that everything has a place and to know where that place is. Just as in the example of adrenalin, which is essentially lethal although it is the hormone that makes us resilient in life and keeps us alive. The wind is the same... Rain drowns us in floods but also gives us life. To touch is the joy of love but it can also bring death. A person speaking might be a sage explaining the secrets of the universe or a garrulous charlatan. The beat of a drum may turn into cacophony at any moment, or the mellifluous sound of the violin can descend into a screech waging war on our eardrums.

However, none of these can change the consequences or operational function of pressure. Pressure is both the insemination and incubation chamber of new beginnings. The universe is a mirror of a thousand faces, which reflects itself into eternity with eternal images. When you think about it, everything we consider to be new is actually a reflection of the universe compressing itself into new shapes over and over again. It is the universe taking a breather and constitutes an important part of its internal dynamics. There is always something being compressed and that will eventually become a piece of existence reflected into the cosmic mirrors. The universe repeats this process like habitual behaviour, and the process of creation, its would-be representative, is constantly renewed. This is the cosmic memory without which nothing could exist - if the cosmic memory was to disappear, so too would the universe.

If we had no memory, then neither the people we love nor our enemies would exist. There would be no-one to love us and no-one for us to hate - no family, no children, no job and no home. Without memory we would have neither a knowledge of our age or any expectation of death. Living without fear would also mean living without love. We could neither plan a holiday nor embrace the person we loved. Without a memory bank, even the most basic object put before us would seem alien - including the beautiful woman gazing deeply into our eyes and the man who makes our knees tremble when he touches our arm.

Likewise, atomic nuclei without any memory keep on shuffling the numbers of neutrons, protons and electrons gathered around them. Even for one element to maintain its existence as the same element, it needs a billion-year memory. You might be able to conceptualise this by imagining that if the atoms and molecules lost their memory, our car engine would suddenly turn into oxygen and then silicon, your seats would suddenly become fluid and the water flowing into your hand from the spring would turn into iron in your hand.

Over the coming chapters, we will look at the universe's memory and the story of hydrogen from different angles. When talking about the universe, it is impossible to avoid the subject coming back to hydrogen again and again. It is like the main actor of a play, always returning to the stage throughout the story. Put simply, in order to be hydrogen and remain as hydrogen, there needs to be one proton within your core and one electron wrapped around you. As long as you follow this recipe, you will be hydrogen. How much capacity you will have to change is also written into your memory. On the other hand, if you have six neutrons, six protons and six electrons, you will be carbon. Carbon exists in this form all across the universe, and hydrogen wanders the entire cosmos as one proton and one electron. Just as we do not leave home in the morning and forget our address, hydrogen does not forget its hydrogenity, nor carbon its innate carbonness. This memory is the force that holds the entire universe together.

However, sometimes the hydrogen's dissolute nature takes the helm, throwing a neutron into its control room and thereby changing its address to deuterium. Molecules all over the universe are formed from atoms connected together in the same string and act in the same manner everywhere. There are some atoms they like to connect to and some that they prefer to avoid. Their memories never fall short of the mark and, just as you recognise who your lover is, they recognise exactly which atoms they will unite with.

Although it may seem like everything in the universe is dancing recklessly at an endless party, with the exception of a few rogue visitors, nobody takes anyone's lover away from them. Everything attracts pushes and pulls something, but the atom does not have a core that encircles and traps neutrons and protons. The neutron and proton connect with such an intense nuclear force that to break this bond requires the atom bomb. In the same way, electrons push each other so much that each one is dispersed to the far corners of the universe without any external force pulling them there. In summary, everything is established using energy and the universe forgets nothing, which is how it has maintained its existence for 14 billion years.

RECORDING

Although when I first met her, it occurred to me to give her money, I hesitated because there was something in her behaviour that made me uneasy. Her harsh looks, that contrasted with the soft, bulging lines of her huge body, seemed to bore through the strollers in the park and gaze on into the distance. Part of the long bench where she sat was covered by two boxes containing her belongings and she was constantly mumbling to herself. I went towards her. Her chubby hands were cracked from cold and dirt. It was as if her fingers had been covered in matt paint encompassing all the tones of black and purple and were immune to the bitingly cold breeze. Muttering under her breath, she had started to write something in neat handwriting on the lined notepad on her lap. When I asked her what he was writing, she lifted her head slightly to look at me. Her cheeks, puffed and purple with cold, also seemed oblivious to the wind stinging her skin. I was surprised to see that her eyebrows were sketched carefully, almost like a bow. The clear skies and piercing cold of February seemed to be reflected in the depths of her ashen eyes.
Without pausing to think, she said,

'A petition.'

'Who are you writing to?' I asked.

'To God,' she replied, 'The Great Judge.'

I was intrigued by her answers and my curiosity was aroused.

'How many pages is this petition?' I asked.

She raised her head and peered at me. She thought for a while before replying in a voice, croaky and hoarse from cigarettes and cold,

'Sir, I don't want to bother you. It's 600 pages. I photocopy it in the bookshop on the corner and keep a copy there. When I finish it, I'm going to send it to the Judge,' she continued.

She spoke very politely, addressing me as 'sir' in almost every sentence. She agreed to let me look at her work and I read about 10 pages of it with great interest. For some reason or other, perhaps because of my dark navy suit or shiny black shoes, she seemed to trust me. She continued confidentially, as if sharing a secret,

'Actually, I don't really trust the bookshop - they want to make some money from my book, but I don't have anyone else to leave it with.'

Here was a woman living in a park, writing a request to the Great Judge and storing it away in plastic carrier bags, while at the same time making spare copies in case it got wet in the rain. As I read on, it was not just her neat handwriting that impressed me, but also her mastery of vocabulary and grammar. However, reading the well-formed and enthralling sentences, which seemed in the main to be unconnected to one another, threw my mind into a quandary. It was like trying to solve a sequence of cryptic clues. The ebbs and flows that had shaped her life and outlook spilled out on the pages before me.

She suffered from schizophrenia. The penny dropped - she was writing her experiences and decoding them for all to understand as if it was her sacred duty. I began to feel ashamed that I had belittled the woman with my meaningless presumptions. I felt as if I was on the edge of a precipice, looking into space. The woman's writing was still in my hands. What she was trying to do was no trivial act. I brought her my own writing. Every corner of my home and every drawer of my office desk was covered in papers and notepads full of scribbled notes. I wracked my brains to find a difference between our respective projects, but could find nothing. We were both doing exactly the same thing. We were bearing witness to our experience of life and recording the waves of life's great ocean, host to trillions of creatures and processes, that had broken on our tiny shores.

Keeping a personal notebook is one of the first things that children think of doing and most of us have kept one at some point, even if for a brief period of time. These days, it is Facebook that helps us satiate our desire to keep up with our friend's adventures and share photos of the sights and journeys that fill our lives. Life's every smile, celebration and emotion hangs on our Facebook wall. The day we learnt how to make tools and weapons, we began carving our experiences and our feats against the mammoths into the cave walls. It was 30,000 years ago and at that time we could only communicate with a few sounds and symbols.

Perhaps the act of recording was the universe's way of being, from where it reproduced knowledge. Perhaps this is why knowledge is life's most sacred treasure trove - it is the same age as the universe and probably it's way of being. As for the brain, perhaps that is our own tiny mirror into which this knowledge is reflected for us. Rather than being the great discovery that humans boast of, knowledge simply gazes through our window like one character in our cosmic process. God has thousands of names and cosmic life should have just as many, because whenever we look at it, we see it in a multitude of semblances although it is in fact always the same.

Every new formation is in fact a new record, and every new record completes the weave of history. As long as the universe keeps going, no process will stop. In our life, there is no such thing as attaining one's desire. Our every moment creates another moment and we do not exist simply in the current moment of our existence, but rather within our whole existence. Looked at in this light, we can see that the past is neither destroyed or forgotten. If this wasn't the case and the past was destroyed in the same way that some of our memories are forgotten, the wall we built today would turn into a scattered pile of rubble tomorrow, then become hot lava and lose the disintegrating atoms and electrons, transforming into everything's essence. The things we did yesterday are still with us, thousand-year stone walls are still standing and the planets and sun around us have been with us for millions of years, which means that the links in the chain of the past are still very much with us. Time is the universe's fourth dimension and as long as the universe exists, it will continue to expand by continually adding a new line to enrich the sketch. The universe and time move forward wrapped up inside each other and by morphing into each other.

14 billion years ago today, when the universe was too hot to sustain individual existence and separation, it was a thick slurry. The temperature, which had exceeded trillions of degrees (10^{32}°C), was dropping to one billion degrees in tiny fractions of a second.

Put another way, the universe was up to 10 trillion x 10 trillion times hotter than the red-hot core of the sun and cooling rapidly as it expanded. As far as we know, quarks, one of the smallest building blocks of existence, were continually darting around inside the puzzle. The quarks clashed with their antiquarks time and time again. They were so squashed in that they wondered how they could find any more space to clash in. Suddenly, the quarks noticed something - time had begun to record everything.

From that moment on, as long as time itself continued, every step of every quark would exist together with time. It did not forget - it remembered.

Sometime later, one up quark began to dance with a down quark. As they had no certificate of birth at the time, these were the names they gave each other. They had no unique names as individualism had not yet been - there was no empty space to be individualised anyway. We still address the quarks like this today, in memory of that time; but as for us, the fruits of their fine weaving, we all now have our individual names. The load of the up quarks was +2/3 and that of the down antiquarks was +1/3; so both of them together made +1. They were overjoyed when they noticed this - they were finally complete. In dedication to the dance of that day, we still describe couples in love as 'making each other complete', or like 'two halves of an apple'.

However, their togetherness did not last long and soon disintegrated. Scattering energy all around themselves, they turned into photons. The photons glowed and then mixed in with each other. From that day on, love was always that way. It would appear suddenly and later the lights would dissipate, bringing it to an end. No-one would ever know where love had gone. Just as today, still nobody knows. Suddenly, a spark reflected into our eyes is ignited. Later on it goes just as it came, but striking us with it energy on the way.

This was the first cosmic existence experiment. Love was the first step to ensure the survival of the various species. With its first step, the universe must have tried the process of creating existence through pairing. The pieces found each other and later separated like two figures on a dance floor. They were couples that came together, perhaps thousands or even billions of times, to create a being, no different to ourselves. We always look at each other, and when our eyes meet, they dart away. As we walk along the path, our existence makes contact with hundreds of people and changes its mind hundreds of times. It is said that the length of time that quarks stay together is close to one billionth of a second. But what can we do? The important thing is to come together and live that moment.

Cosmic behaviour and the establishment of the cosmic structure defined itself in this way in the first split seconds. From that moment on, no matter where we look, this is the behaviour we see.
This structure, which consists of two quarks that are connected by the adhesive spirit called gluon and immediately decays, is referred to by physicists as pi meson, or pion for short. The recording was in progress. From then on, every new step would continue to be reflected, hidden between the light waves, in trillions of cosmic mirrors. Even if we could not see the image in the mirror, children, lunatics and mystics would observe it and smile. And the physicists...

After a tenth of the universe's first second, pressure dropped, the temperature fell to 30 trillion degrees and the quarks relaxed, this time forming three way connections. Physicists called this new formation neutrons and protons. However, the universe was so hot and compacted (akin to 30 times the energy density of water) that the never-ending particle collisions did not leave the neutrons as neutrons, nor the protons as protons; the neutrons and protons were constantly turning into each other. Still, if nothing else, the quarks had learnt to connect in threes and exist as neutron-protons.

The universe was expanding and writing new information into each new space that opened, as if to make sure it would never forget. It was colliding and learning. Could it be that the expression 'to knock something into someone's head' derived from here? Why not? I think this was our first learning technique. After a while, the adhesive spirit called gluon connected the quarks so tightly that the neutrons and protons assumed a structure that was so strong it could not be broken. The electrons and positrons, who now went everywhere arm in arm not allowing anyone to make a move on them, eventually consumed each other leaving only a few electrons behind. Density had eased, pressure fell and the heat dropped to a bearable heat temperature.

This was the time to learn more and discover new things. Single movement began. Once the confusion lessened and the pressure was lifted, individual movement arose. This was the moment when individual choice and behaviour, the phenomenon we call freedom, began.

Later, the three-quark protons caught the electrons passing by and the electrons swathed the protons. Thus, hydrogen, the world's first element, was born. Fourteen billion years passed from that moment until the present day. The universe may have been in existence for 14 billion years, constantly growing at the same speed, but whenever an electron swathed a three-quark proton, it would be called hydrogen and would always behave as hydrogen. Nothing more and nothing less...

As the world's first element, hydrogen, and later its successors, would bear witness to the cosmic journey. It was the first fertilised cell to develop in the cosmic uterus and its journey is our journey. The changes it has undergone are our changes. Its tendencies are also our tendencies. If we want to understand ourselves, or more to the point, understand life, we first of all need to understand hydrogen. Just as it remembered how to be hydrogen, the universe also retained everything else in its memory: chaos, collision, pressure and release... As well as being the data necessary for hydrogen, these were carried to the furthest corners of the universe.

The universe's route was no easy one. On the road to the unknown territory of the Big Bang, everything was new and the cosmos had no infrastructure capable of making a choice. Like a child lost in the forest, the universe established its own life and corrected itself. However, this was in essence a single life and it was solitary in itself. It is for this reason that the universe is simple. It always repeats what it has learnt and rehashes its past until time brings new knowledge and new highways. Everything that befalls it remains as an unfading reflection in its mirrors.

REflECTIONS

As we touched upon earlier, several hundred thousand years after the Big Bang, when the electrons and positrons that covered everything like swamp mud destroyed each other, existence came about and started to breathe comfortably. The electron-positron shield had gone and the light particles (photons) carrying electromagnetic force could spread freely, filling the entire skies like the migratory birds that herald the start of spring. The temperature had dropped to 3,000 degrees and the universe continued to cool as it expanded. The radiation that appeared and began to spread on that day cooled more each day, but together with the universe, it shrouded every part of the cosmos. It seems that it cooled in tangent with the cosmos and reached as far as the cosmos reached.

One day, two scientists noticed the radiation that covered every inch of the universe. First of all, they didn't recognise it - the photons had significantly aged. Their 3,000-degree entity was only 2.7 degrees above absolute zero, but they were still the same radiation. They had not disappeared but were all over the cosmos, about 400 million in each cubic metre. These were the photons that had been set free at the end of the repressive regime of the electrons 14 billion years ago. In fact, you are familiar with them. If you leave the TV on by accident when broadcasting has closed for the night, the tiny crackles of popcorn that flicker on the screen and are referred to as snow are the same photons that astronomers and physicists call ' cosmic microwave background radiation'. The minute photons that lived 14 billion years ago are winking at us in the early hours of the morning.

Perhaps we should never forget that everything in existence today is waving at us from beyond our billion year past and, bearing in mind that nothing disappears, perhaps we should live a little more carefully. You can say that something is forgotten, but nothing, be it malicious or favourable, completely leaves us - just as we cannot really repair damage by simply uttering the words sorry and forgive me. We are reminded of this somewhat in the old adage, 'Give a dog a bad name and hang him.' Is there anyone who can leave their past behind them like a buried, disintegrated detail? Our every word, act and choice stays with us like a label we cannot remove. Even if we later think they are forgotten, they will still be reflected in our mirror.

In our life, there is no changing your mind and turning back the clock. We can only change our direction. We have another saying for this, 'A fault confessed is half redressed.' In short, a consequence-free mistake is not possible in this universe. There can be neither malice without repercussions nor goodness without reward. But the universe's Law of Correspondences does not much resemble the anticipations of our cultural archive. Sometimes, the consequence of our wrongdoing is simply our neighbours turning the other way when we pass and the reward for the greatest act of kindness is simply a huge smile.

If we look at the universe and want to converse with it, we must throw off our cultural identity and adopt that of our interlocutor. It's language and etiquette are different. We look through a window of 30-40 or 60-70 years, widening it to 4,000-5,000 years if we add the writings of our ancestors, but its window goes back 14 billion years. Perhaps by approaching life with such simplicity, Sufis and Buddhist monks are experimenting with the language of the universe. In fact, today our property and wealth are fulfilling the same function as the electrons in the first few hundred thousand years of the cosmos. Everything we have is connected to them and can only form within them. We cannot breathe inside the energy of money and affluence. Our every movement collides with them. We are so separated from our past by their opium that we cannot even imagine a life without money and wealth. Maybe that is why people think Sufis are crazy.

Nevertheless we can feel the multitude of reflections from the universe within our ego. We may not see them exactly, but it seems as if we know what they are when our fingertips touch them.

For example, any sort of explosion, either social, psychological or physical, is immediately followed by a period in which no laws, rules or institutions function and no equation yields results. For 10 to the minus 43 seconds after the Big Bang, chaos reigned and there were no rules governing what happened. Afterwards, the universe's four main forces separated and defined themselves; the foundation came much later - just like the initial days of a huge revolt.

No matter how organized it may have been, a revolt is a revolt and its outbreak is a period of lawlessness. So much so that it can even swing in the opposite direction to that aimed for by the rebels. Whatever lays behind the revolt, one of the first consequences is always pillage and rape. Windows are smashed, houses set alight and cars burnt out. In this period, no act is out of bounds. The local shopkeeper, that you have been greeting every day on your way home or your neighbour two doors down may turn out to be your attacker. However intense the interior pressure is before the explosion, the ensuing temperature, together with the paralysis of time which causes it to break all its links, will be equally powerful. However great the pressure, the effect of the explosion after the structure cracks will be equally great, leading into a period of emergency law, which means in other words that laws do not apply. (Strangely, this situation has even entered our legislation like a joke; for example, when parliament declares a state of emergency, scores of laws are suspended.)

The fault lines under Haiti were so taut with compression and under such intense pressure that when they broke, they caused a devastating scale nine earthquake. The ground was torn up by the huge energy released and 250,000 people died, while 1.5 million were left homeless. In reality, it was simply severely compressed energy cracking and dispersing - the visible physical impact of this energy. In such circumstances, there is another destructive phenomenon running alongside and that is all kinds of violation, including pillage and those of a sexual nature. In Haiti, women and girls as young as ten fled to the refuges and camps, but could not flee the rapists. They had done no harm to anyone, nor were they in any state to communicate sexual signals to anyone. They were just dusty and destitute. We won't look any more into the reasons behind this savagery, because the paralysis of existing laws in this period is a reflection left in our mirror by the occurrences in the universe's first moment. The only thing that all huge discharges of energy have in common is disorder. It is a time of conflict, violation and lawlessness. Whatever name is given to the explosion, compressed energy always behaves in the same way when it discharges.

In Russia 1917, the old Tsarist regime was overthrown ushering in a new era; the significance of this revolution was not the overthrow of the tsar, but the destruction of the dominant global economic and social system and the introduction of a new order in Russia. Under such circumstances, it was normal for the ruling class of capitalists and aristocrats to suffer, but the entire population were burned by the fire of revolution for a long time. People tried to protect themselves against violence and attack by setting up apartment committees and hiring unemployed soldiers. This was a political revolution, and it was therefore incomprehensible that some saw it as an opportunity to brutalise others. The political class thought that everything would settle once they took power, but the revolution continued to destroy and take lives until its energy had sufficiently reduced.

Just as you cannot say to a hurricane, 'Our job is done now, so stop', the same is valid for revolutions. When societal repression reaches its final peak, a revolution is its exploding energy and the end of the violence depends on the rules of nature, just as with hurricanes and earthquakes. In actual fact, with the exception of Stalin, all the leaders of the revolution experienced immense suffering and were exterminated one by one, sometimes even by each other. Is it realistic to ascribe the degeneration of this momentous event and its loyal cadre to the merciless calculations of a mere mortal called Stalin? When the 30 year repressive regime of Hüsnü Mübarek in Egypt was overthrown by a huge people's movement, why is it that women were raped and the Cairo museum was looted, leaving behind shattered statues and dismembered mummies.

Likewise, in Tunisia, after the people's movement achieved its aim by removing the state dictator, a restoration of calm was expected. However, how can you explain the fact that events continued to spill onto the streets as unions and others withdrew from the council? How is it that almost 100,000 people died in bombing and chaos after the deposition of Saddam Hussein, who had crushed and silenced people for decade? The upheaval left a taste of freedom, but the chaos continued for years to come. And how about the French Revolution? Why did the terror and unrest continue after the king was beheaded and the revolutionary leaders turn on each other? Was it just the downside of human nature? If that's the case, where did this barbaric nature hide itself until 1789. Why did people who had been neighbours, living amicably side-by-side with no problems, start to attack each other and why couldn't this malice be stopped?

There could only be one explanation for this. Eventually, regardless of whether the root cause is physical or social, the extreme pressure created by repressive regimes, and all structures that apply pressure, shatters the energy that is containing it and explodes. Every great explosion temporarily paralyzes its environment and during this period no laws are in operation. Everything unfolds of its own accord, projecting into all elements of the life around it and heading for collision. Collision is not an aim, but rather a part of the disorder ushered in by the new development. This continues until the energy density has fallen beneath a certain level. Indeed, all the revolutions in history have unfolded in this way. Now let's leave aside public life and return to our private lives.

We share our lives and share the same bed for decades; but after every difficulty and restriction we place in our respective lives, even those in the name of love, eventually the day comes when life becomes unbearable. In the end, one of us says,' That's it.' When that moment comes and the words are said, what ensues? First your partner's face colour changes. The blood drains from their face, leaving a frenzied expression. The words seem unbelievable. The door has been opened, but the inside pressure has still not discharged into the vacant space. A thousand questions rush through your head and every answer is immediately deleted. After a while (the time is relative - it could be a minute or a whole week later), you see the first lights of the explosion in their eyes. The pressure has emptied into the vacant space behind the door. Suddenly you are faced with an unrecognisable person - a fire-breathing dragon that burns you and everything around you with its flames, a monster that is not perturbed from torching its environment even if it hurts itself at the same time.

It's not just long-term marriage that can produce this effect; any long-term affection can yield the same result. The phenomenon is simply constricted, suppressed energy, spilling through the door that has opened. No-one is a monster - neither man nor woman. The all-consuming flames and storms that tear up your familiar world are the energy that has built up inside for years without you even noticing, just like the eruption of a volcano. Repression and our inner accumulation certainly don't begin with malicious intent. Sometimes, we even inflict this on ourselves and those we are close to because we love them. Sometime later, our love becomes a monster for both us and our families.

Although people and their characteristics change according to social environment, there is a classic relationship model that varies very little. Generally, love envelops us so much that we don't notice how much we are in the midst of this classic cycle. We feel as if the relationship is unique to us. The following story shares some of these features.

Ramiz was an associate professor. Selda was studying at the same university and was one of Ramiz's students. While completing her final thesis, she continually consulted with Ramiz and he did his best to help her out. A while later, they began to go to the cafe opposite the university to discuss the progress of the thesis. Then at lunchtime, Selda went shopping with Ramiz, ostensibly to help him choose a shirt, and one week later she went to Ramiz's place for breakfast. She was steeped in admiration for her teacher and he infatuated by her.

After they got married, they began to get to know each other properly. They had to adapt to each other due to the numerous personal characteristics they had not noticed or not thought important before. Ramiz had some issues he found hard to overcome when living with a woman. First of all Selda's skirt hemline was dropped by 3 cm, then by 10 cm. Ramiz wanted her to be comfortable and content with him, but what would a few extra centimetres on the hemline actually change? Later Selda sensed that Ramiz was fed up with the male friends that came to visit her and even jealous. They were old friends, soulmates, that she loved to be with, but it wasn't worth upsetting Ramiz. She began to start meeting her school friends away from home. In any case, she had started a new job and hardly had time to take a breath. Gradually, the meetings with friends became more infrequent, eventually being replaced by forwarding silly stories over email. Her only friends were now Ramiz's married friends from the university.

Three years later, their first child came along and she took six months unpaid leave to be with her child. Before she was able to return to work, the bank she had been working for collapsed in an economic crisis, leaving her nowhere to return to. Nine other banks had collapsed at the same time and the jobs market was flooded with those looking for work. There was no way she could find a new job now. After almost 20 job applications, she still had no luck. Meanwhile, Ramiz had become a professor as well as writing the daily economy column for a huge national newspaper and appearing once a week on a TV economy programme. As they had no need for extra income, at the suggestion of Ramiz, she postponed her employment search.

By the time their daughter started school, the years Selda had spent away from her career closed all the doors to her return. Instead, she threw herself into the role of full-time housewife. In the morning, she got the kids ready for school; towards midday she walked the cute dogs with their huge ears almost flopping on the ground and occasionally met her female school friends for lunch. She had virtually no free time. There were just two people and a dog necessary to make her happy. Although at times she wondered if there was anything she actually did just for herself, she didn't dwell on it too much. She saw herself as the engine driving a 4-person family, which would never break down.

As she was worried about her daughter's future, they sent her to a costly private school renowned for its superior standards. The fees, that were not far off the salary of a mid-level manager, squeezed the household budget. Selda countered this with personal self-sacrifice and tried to cut back her spending whenever possible. She changed her hairdresser and began buying cheaper brands of make-up and perfume. Her previously favoured creams, that each cost a small fortune, were replaced by cheaper versions such as apricot oil and glycerine. Much as she wanted her sacrifice to be recognised, nobody noticed the changes she had made. The occasional intimations she dropped into conversation hung in the air, unnoticed.

At home, she was like a live-in servant. Dialogue with her husband rarely extended beyond,
' What's for dinner? How's our girl? The electricity bill has arrived...', and other similar banal topics.

Sometimes, as she stirred the soup in the kitchen, she thought long and hard about the life she was living. At one time, Ramiz had been her thesis supervisor rather than her husband, and as much as she had lofty ideals, she also wondered how far away the relationship between them had drifted from its magical beginnings. Now it seemed as if the exciting life in which they had scattered sparks all around them was buried, leaving a mundane existence in which the unremarkable days were dismissed without a thought.

In fact, nothing had been lost. Selda had buried every desire, aim and goal in a cavernous well inside her. Nothing was completely destroyed. It was life's refuse collection service and she threw everything of her own into there, locked it up tightly, then used everything of Ramiz's in its place. She had incarcerated her desires and inner energies. When Ramiz told her he was in love with another woman and wanted a divorce, Selda couldn't believe the words echoing in her ears. Suddenly, she felt she had fallen into a deep whirlpool in which the myriad of words and concepts she knew of were tangled together. Her head was spinning. Her hands found the arms of the sofa next to her and she crumbled into it. She looked at him, motionless...

That evening she threw Ramiz out. The following day, she gathered up all of his possessions, threw them out of the window and spent the rest of the day in fits of tears. The next morning, she stood outside the bank waiting for it to open. She emptied their joint account and transferred all the money into a new account she had opened for herself. She was determined to see Ramiz burn in the fires of hell. She went to see a lawyer friend and asked,

'Tell me how I can damage his academic career - I want his head to swing!'

She was unrecognisable now; her eyes were circled with purple and her facial expression had a demonic quality to it. She later proved that Ramiz had been collaborating with investment companies, using the comments and interpretations he broadcast on the TV or in his news columns to manipulate markets for the benefit of stock market players. When he was convicted, he also lost his job at the university. However, all the money she had taken from the joint accounts was also confiscated by the court. Along with Ramiz, the general manager of the stock exchange company, and the journalist's economy page director were also convicted and unemployed. The fire engulfed everything around it, even the children. Undoubtedly, that was not Selda's intention. But only a huge explosion could set her free after 13 years of suppressing her inner energies for the sake of the family's happiness and future. She would burn everything around her.

Why did our ancestors come up with the saying, 'An iron fist in a velvet glove.'? It must have been borne from collective experience over the centuries. However, an iron fist is not necessarily fatal. Energy does as it pleases and does not leave its tomorrows until the next day or the day after next. The laws of physics apply everywhere. How could we even consider that the laws that created the great universe would not in some way affect us and our miniscule relationships.

The moral of the story is that sacrifice is not a good thing. Don't let this happen to you. Despite how voluntary it may be, every sacrifice is another bullet in the barrel of a gun. It's not clear who will bear the brunt when the trigger is pulled one day. However, as much as the directionless feelings that have built up inside you can be a blight on your future life, they can also be the rocket fuel that shoots you into the stars. This is the flip side of the coin.

MIXTURE

The universe has two faces - just like a coin. One observes and the other one writes. One fills and the other empties. One saves and the other spends. One loves and the other one hates. One turns the world into hell and the other creates thousands of romantic nights. In this way, two faces turn into thousands of faces behind which a new door opens. At the same time, the resources of a new beginning are being gathered together. Every step towards the future is just the movement of accumulated energy in the newly opened streams.

The universe is still continuing its journey that began with the spurting forth and scattering of compressed, accumulated energy. As you can see, pressure is not all bad. It is the gestation period of our existence. It is also the brush that gives colour to our behaviour. We walk back and forth, always returning to pressure and tension. Just as we say 'same garment, different cloth', most stories of the universe are dressed in the same pressure and tension. As for us, as we go back and forth, in every mirror we glimpse another depiction of tension.

Neither Vivaldi's emotional transmission nor Paganini's unholy talents would have reached us without the taut strings of a violin. Even five-year olds must know how much tension there needs to be in a shrivelled piece of leather in order to turn it into a shaman's drum. No-one would doubt that without tensing the bow, an arrow would not travel much further than a metre.
Can there be combat without anger? Indeed, repression and tension are not always bad things.
Now, let's return to our journey.

As the clash of electrons and positrons that dominated the universe came to an end, there were very few electrons left. When the temperature became low enough to allow breathing, there was a huge celebration. New pairs added to the electron-positron coupling that made the first dance, and at the end of this cosmic dance party, everywhere was covered in a hydrogen cloud. The inebriated protons began to flirt with the neutrons sitting unassumedly in the corner. By the end of the party, deuterium and tritium, both types of hydrogen, came into existence along with surplus helium. However, the clouds emanating from the dance party had grown considerably, becoming denser and denser under the effects of gravity. As their density increased, they pulled other clouds towards them to become even denser. They formed the first metropoles of the new order. Just like every great mass, every metropolis* becomes a repressive force for those living inside it. Like it or not, you cannot escape to lead your own life peacefully. It was the same back at the beginning; hydrogen atoms were crushed and crushed under the pressure of this great mass. As the pressure grew, the hydrogen forming particles trembled and the more they shook, the hotter the heat they gave off.

(*) Footnote: In fact, we have similar experiences due to the pressure and tension created by the endless succession of decisions in our major cities. Sadly, our decision process begins early in the morning. First of all, as the early morning alarm clock screams at us, we decide whether to snooze it and dose for another five minutes. In just five minutes, we are once more torn between the temptation of staying in bed or snoozing it again. The next decisions are whether to take a shower and which clothes to wear. We browse our clothes, unable to decide which one is the right choice for the day. Men have the angst of selecting an appropriate tie. Perhaps the choice between having breakfast at home or the local snack bar is the easiest. Which pair of shoes goes best with our outfit? Once on the street, there are more decisions to be made. One of the biggest conundrums of our day is how best to bypass the morning rush hour traffic. You can imagine the stream of fast, difficult decisions we have to make once we are finally seated at our desks Wherever there is density and pressure, there is heat in its wake, followed by movement. Even our dreams are full to bursting point. This is the rhythm of city dwellers. No city dweller has the luxury of sitting under a tree until evening gazing at the view. Even our meditation is measured in minutes, not to mention our sexual encounters. However, we should remember that all innovations are not just dreamt of in the cities, but also created. Pressure primes us for new developments. Metropoles are like farms where hundreds of thousands of chickens are hatching and every pressure that necessitates a decision is pregnant with a new birth. On the other hand, the shepherd waking up on the mountain only has one significant decision to make: whether to take the sheep to the hill on the left or the hill on the right for grazing. Once the decision is made, there will be no more important decisions that day.

The warm environment created the universe's first incubation period. During this incubation period, hydrogen, which had avoided the fires of hell, created multitudes of new formations as the protons in the structure of deuterium and helium separated. Each new formation was a different egg. Just as fish scatter their eggs to the bottom of the sea, hydrogen and helium began to scatter their eggs into a new hydrogen star. The elements and heavy metals we know today came about in this incubation period and, like everything else around us, they did not forget their unique personalities. The iron that first occurred billions of years ago is exactly the same today. The copper is still the same copper. The universe was learning in the process of creating and this is how it was bringing new creations into the world.

As we know, the inside of the womb is warm, and during incubation the eggs need to be kept warm. The people we prefer to be with are 'warm'. People we take a dislike to are 'cold'. The body becomes hot during mating. When we are afraid, we are 'frozen'. We are happy when we receive a 'warm' look, but not a 'frosty' stare. Another way of referring to affectionate feelings is to 'warm to someone'. Seeds split open and grow when the weather warms up. Trees grow faster in warmer climes.

Hydrogen needed a warm environment in order to form gold, platinum, iron and other elements. As it made random new structures by reuniting the disintegrating subatomic particles, the star was densifying more and more, its mass becoming more compressed and shrunken. Eventually, it was unable to cope with the pressure and exploded, spurting out its contents to the furthest corners of the cosmos, as it had learnt from its mother, the universe. This is how the hydrogen star scattered its offspring across the universe. The others did the same, scattering heavy metals and other elements to the far corners of the universe, where they entered the gravitational field of other stars and various large clouds and took up home there. They mixed in with the world, which at that time was a cloud, and waited for new lives to be born.

You know that mixing is good. More accurately speaking, it is a familiar process. We mix our tea with sugar and our coffee with milk. We make a mixed stew of courgette, aubergine and potatoes. We don't make mashed potato without mixing in a little water. How many meals do we eat without adding salt and pepper? The bee gathers pollen from all the bees it can find and services the tiny honeycomb cells. We don't condone marriage within the family; the bride and groom should certainly be from different families and we all agree that hybrids are the most beautiful. Chemists are continually mixing up concoctions in their laboratories, just like their alchemist ancestors. School is not just one lesson - we learn about maths, but also music and history. It is not unknown for physics students to do a master's degree in business administration. We desire to speak more than one language.

We mix together the things we see and the things we experience. This is why we travel and when we go on holiday, we head for somewhere different. If we choose to commit to a lifelong partnership, we envy those whose experience is a bit more varied. We could not reproduce by copying ourselves. Every new being is a mixture resulting from a male fertilising a female. Our instinct is to mix things up. Apart from following in the footsteps of our ancestors, this instinct is also one of the building blocks of our existence and an inheritance from the formation of the universe.

We are not impressed by one-sided people and describe them as colourless or one-dimensional. Diversity is a characteristic of the universe, which means it is also characteristic of us and we shouldn't shy away from it. Every stretch of water requires a different type of vessel to navigate it - one type for shallow, rocky waters and another type for deep, choppy waters. Bring yourself into harmony with this life... Don't live in mono. You should have a thousand sides, a thousand types of love and a thousand types of hate. With a thousand types of vessel, you can be sure you will never sink and can get to any place you desire.

By allowing ourselves to mix, we avoid both shutting ourselves off from the reality of existence and becoming buried in ourselves. To mix is to desist from attempting to establish a different structure from the universe, which is another part of our existence. It is to completely accept all the movement of the universe inside our existence and live in harmony with all forces of the universe. It is to be open to everything. The great economic theory of liberalism says: 'Let it go. Let it pass'. In other words, let it be or leave things alone. Just like the famous Beatles song, 'Let it be'.

The message in essence is that we should not interfere, but rather leave the universe to do as it knows best. Anything that is closed up and isolated from its environment will rot. The process of rotting is a particular form of disintegration and scattering. Even gossip has a positive side. To gossip is to free oneself from keeping inner secrets and allow others to prize them from you as they wish. Perhaps that is why researchers say gossip is good for your health. The windows of the house need to be left open so that air can circulate freely inside. The curtains should be open to allow the sun to enter. When at home, don't shut yourself off from the blue sky and pretty clouds in the daytime, or the glitter of the stars at night.

In your relationships with others, don't keep yourself hidden and shut off your access roads. Don't create lifelong resentments or make sweeping promises. You will either rot inside or the forces of the universe will eventually crush your decisions and promises. Disintegrated promises will damage you and those around you as much as every disintegrating object damages its environment. You were not the creator of the universe and therefore you should desist from trying to challenge its principles. Every challenge is sentenced to fail in the face of life. Never forget that everything you challenge is a part of life with 14 billion years of history behind it. In conclusion, we can see that pressure and tension are beneficial to a degree, but they become detrimental when applied too much. This is how the universe always learnt. Pressure gave birth to creativity, but also the incredible force that is part of its natural make-up. Pressure generates energy.

We should remember that if we want to purchase something, we need to have enough money on us. The words of Nasreddin Hoca on this subject, express this universal truth in the purest way.

'The one who pays the piper, plays the tune.'

There is no object or moment that does not come with a price. The cosmos formed out of energy of its own accord, and therefore the valid currency is energy. Everything is formed from energy and moves with energy. Energy moves your car. If you pay the piper you get to hear your tune.

Give the order and get it done.
Give the money and use it.
Give interest and be loved.
Give water and fertilizer and make it grow.
Feed and take its milk.

You can carry on with your own examples...

But if we ask ourselves what energy actually is, perhaps we should first write Einstein's formula: $E=mc^2$. Basically, it means that if you multiply the amount of mass by the speed of light squared, it will be equal to its energy; in other words, where there is mass, there is energy. Whether a mass is solid or soft, the subatomic particles that it consists of take energy from each other in order to maintain its structure while the electrons continue to buzz in their environment. Every chemical reaction is in fact a tale of energy exchange and every thought in our head is a chemical and electrical occurrence.

Basically, as we live, speak, eat, love, laugh or cry, energy bubbles inside us at different frequencies and we are also a receptor for energy from others. We hang on to some of the energy flowing over us, while some of it just glances off us and continues on its way. Happy-go-lucky types reflect it their mirrors, but anxious types soak it up like a sponge. We previously remarked that the energy accumulated inside us could fuel an engine to take us to the stars.

At every moment of our life, we are absorbing things from life - be they good or bad - and they are all forms of energy. Without even noticing what we are taking in, we fill up just like a dam taking in water. If our walls are not robust enough, we will break down and scatter the contents, damaging both ourselves and our environment. This is our genetic inheritance. Only the universe knows which of us has walls strong enough to resist; we cannot know what is delicately inscribed into our genetic codes. Some of our walls cannot cope with the pressure of education and break up at that stage, while others of us internalise all kinds of troubles, imprisoning ourselves with them unless one day a door opens inside and we let it all out in a flash. Or sometimes it can happen gradually, without burning and smashing the world around us, by making pictures, writing words or music to release the accumulation. Is there a balladeer in the world that has not experienced pain? Among the works of art that touch us most deeply, how many of their creators were born into a happy existence, lived happily, cushioned by their family's feather beds and learned of the world through the eyes of a private tutor? In order to switch on the piercing light inside, a person should experience the ache of love if nothing else.

We are all made differently and reflect the universe in different ways. For some of us, the reflection of light dazzles with its brilliance and then suddenly disappears. For others, it seems to grow imperceptibly accumulating as if in a hidden battery, following which it begins to give off a lifelong glow. Some earn a Nobel prize, some become industrial magnates and others property tycoons. However, this torch is not one that is passed from father to child. To earn or win success is different to the act of managing it, and the children of winners can only try to manage it. But it is hard to keep masses of accumulated force in one place and most empires disintegrate at the hands of following generations.

This is what is meant by chance - it is your ability to gather and accumulate light. Astrologers say the same thing in a different way. Every one of us has a different battery, energy collector and discharging mechanism. We release energy in different amounts. If the in-out mechanism of our collector or battery is not compatible, the result is different depending on the nature of the incompatibility. Our life was established on the balance of receiving and giving. We earn and we relinquish. We are loved and we love. Although we don't try to imprison the air inside us during the breathing process, our internal metabolism becomes miserly when it comes to an outside exchange, and we leave our natural balance. We plunder and steal. Our craving advances without limit. For this reason, even if our body has a healthy existence, our societal life is full of blocked, explosive relationships and lives.

Some earn a fortune but strangely enough end up with nothing in the end. Some earn very little but live prosperously of their own means. In spite of their huge earnings and great prosperity, some people are one day faced with bankruptcy and lose everything. Then, the same cycle begins all over again. For others, no matter how hard they struggle, they are only ever able to put food on the table and frequently go hungry. This applies to love as much as it does to material wealth. The most well-known example is that, for some people, lovers are like a stream of cars passing down the road. Whether good or bad, they are never alone long enough to take a break. This is how it was for Hazel and Selim. Both believed in the sanctity of the family and the virtue of marriage and bringing up a family. They were both attractive in all ways and both had good careers. However, when they reached their forties, weary with scores of brief relationships lasting barely five months, they asked themselves this question: I wonder where we went wrong. I asked them,

'How much have you accumulated after all those years of working for such huge salaries?'

They said they could not have survived without credit cards. There was nothing they could do about it - that was their fate. Whatever they did, they were not without money or lovers, but they could not hang on to what they had. One possibility is that their entrance and exit channels shared the same dimensions and their barrage could not hold in the water. Our predecessors called this 'barren' and this is how it is known in our public life.

Bonding is one of the universe's oldest habits.

BONDING

As we have said before, quarks bonded in threes to form neutrons and protons, which are the basis of matter. Neutrons and protons bonded to each other and created the atomic nucleus; the electrons attached to the atoms and the atoms attached to each other to create molecules and consequently life itself. Without molecules, there would be no more salt, sugar, carbohydrates, water, carbon - in short, no life.

Bonding allowed us to form the human body, which consists of over 100 trillion cells of 200 different types, 207 bones and 640 muscles. After that, we took up sticks and stones and went out to hunt in groups of 5-10 people. Again, rather than fighting alone, we opted for all the male clan members to assemble together and go out to fight operating a chain of command, just as our bodies did. Time also advances through bonding, connecting yesterday to today and today to tomorrow and joining the current second to the one before and the one after.

Throughout the passage of time, we have never forgotten this habit of bonding: mother-father-child develop a family bond; families living side-by-side develop a neighbourhood and friendship bond; regions, cities and countries develop citizenship or nationality bonds. There is the formation of Asia, Europe, America and all their associated bonds. Eventually, we arrived at the human race - symbols, letters, words, sentences, books... Everything continued to bond with whatever had gone before. With every new connection, we changed and enriched ourselves. It is for this reason that industrial production based on division of labour enabled greater and better creation. Perhaps this is why the global economic order has created such affluence.

Bonding enables everything to exist in a relationship with everything else - it makes us the reason for each other. Even our reproductive system is established on the basis of our attachment to each other - both physically and emotionally. Without bonds, we have no future.
Bonding also gives us a means of using the same thing in a thousand different ways. This is the way of life. Anything with a single use remains stuck in itself, cut off from other factors. Testosterone forms a thousand different paths for the life process within in our bodies. Adrenaline is just the same. To put it more succinctly, our individual adventure of life is decided by the bonds of a few hormones, bonds which have very different functions.

Bonding is the means of existence and way of life of the formation that started 14 billion years ago. Without this process, the universe would not be here. When there is no bonding, there is chaos. We saw this in the first moments of the universe, All chaotic situations occur when the bonds break, leaving existence exposed and naked. We mentioned before that intense pressure and energy can even break atomic bonds, causing existence to search for the future inside new coincidences as it loses its way and process of being. Essentially, when we form bonds, we are sharing our own self. Moreover, by sharing that day and that future, we enrich life itself.

Neutron-proton and electron bonds were the universe's first experiments at existence, and by forming molecules with their bonds, atoms enriched the universe even more. As for us, no matter how much we complain about our bonds, we bring newness to our lives with them.

Additionally, all atoms do not gravitate towards chaos, but are inclined to exist in a steady state. This is why in their final orbit they try to make their number of electrons up to eight, the number of electrons in inert gases such as neon and argon in their steady state.

The six inert gases do not feel the need to bond with anyone during their lifetime. If you like, you can call them hard-hearted, otherwise we can call them independent gases. For the others, their aim is to be like them. Until they complete their final cycle with eight electrons and reach a structure that has no need to bond, they want to join with other atoms and as they do this they give out energy, which lowers their overall energy level. In atomic language, this is referred to as being in a steady state. The descriptions we use for ourselves are not dissimilar. How strange...

When we have a lover or get married, for some reason it is pretty much forbidden to enter into a relationship with anyone else. Even if it was not expressly forbidden, once we fall in love with someone, our eyes see no-one else and our bodies want nothing but that person. Wherever you go in the world, this relationship model is the same. Until we find our partner, we continue to look around. We look around and measure up the suitability of those we find. Of course, most will not suit us, and strangely when referring to those we are not attracted to, we say,

'I didn't feel any electricity.'

In the same situation, atoms say,

'I didn't feel any electrons.'

When we meet someone who sets us alight, even just by touch, we say,

'Our body chemistry is right.'

If atoms are unable to make the electrons in their final orbit up to eight with the electrons of another atom, they cannot even approach that nucleus. In our case, we say,

'They're not my type.'

Have you ever thought about 'your type' or those that aren't your type within this framework?
Unfortunately, the subject doesn't stop there. Every atom attaches in a different way with a different force. Some connections are rigorously strong, while others are looser. For example, the (+) and (-) electrical charge attraction that forms from the connection of metals and non-metals makes it hard to break the ionic bond. It is much easier to separate the covalent bond established by non-metals from sharing electrons. Following suit, we have a belief that people of different characters (opposite poles) have stronger and more lasting relationships.

There is one electron in the final orbit of sodium (Na). For this reason, it is not inclined to join with oxygen, which has six electrons in its final orbit, but rather with Chloride (Cl), which has seven electrons in its final orbit. It passes its one electron to chloride, immediately making salt (NaCl). Salt is one of the most important building blocks that stops our cells from breaking up. In fact, chloride's powerful structure takes the one electron and there is nothing that sodium can do about it. Sodium surrenders itself to chloride and the other NaCl compounds wrap around them. Thus, the married couple become part of society. There are some festivities and then they live together in a family apartment. Just as billions of grains pour from my salt pot, millions of people come together in the cities and flow through their streets.

Indeed, oxygen helps itself out by using two of its six electrons mutually with another oxygen atom, making its final orbit up to eight and forming the O^2 molecule that we breathe in the air. However, in this case, instead of there being a sovereign like ionic NaCl, who captures the electron, this is a share between two characters of equal strength and they connect together with weaker ties compared to the others. Somehow or other, both of their designations take on a solid state. Just like the elements, we sometimes say to our friends:

'I want to settle down now and lead a steady life.'

What we are actually saying is:

'I want to find a partner and exist together with them.'

While we say that, nothing in the universe continues for ever without changing. Just like the way that carbon monoxide (CO) forgets its oath as soon as it sees the first oxygen molecule, bonds with it and forms carbon dioxide (CO2). Although carbon monoxide has no interest in other elements, it has a weakness towards oxygen, because oxygen elements are each other's soulmates. We experience the same kind of crises. Suddenly, a third party enters your life and you hear your partner telling you:

'I love both of you.'

Just like us, all elements and molecules are not exactly the same. Some forge relationships that last until the grave, while others unravel at the first corner. Also, let's not think that it's easy for the elements to form molecules with each other and separate when they feel like it. That is not the case at all; they are just like us in that respect. You shouldn't imagine, especially after reading these pages, that the atoms and molecules that formed our existence would have relationships with each other that are any different to ours.

As well as this, as atoms bond with each other to form molecules, they release energy with the transfer of electrons. When our eyes and lips meet, we turn into a fireball that sends sparks of happiness out into the sky, just like the atoms. However, this is a one-off and only happens when making the bond. No matter how much you love each other, you will not feel the energy enveloping you again. This is why there is just one, very special honeymoon.

The energy you emit is not just in the light that beams from your eyes; no matter how much money you spend, you hardly notice it. You buy your lover a myriad of gifts - necklaces, earrings, silk scarves or a new shirt and tie etc. You make surprise holiday bookings for the two of you. You go out for meals and are happy to pay the bill. If you need to furnish the house, you spend a fortune and even get into debt. By two years into your relationship, no-one could get you to do even half of that again. So what has changed?

Nothing...But you need to understand that when you make bonds, energy is discharged during the exchange of electrons. To expect the same thing two years later is to put yourself under unnecessary pressure. You cannot take what doesn't exist. On the other hand, the phenomenon has another aspect to it. Atoms that have over four electrons in their final orbit, take electrons from their partners in order to take on a steady state. Those with less than four atoms are always giving.

Doesn't this remind you slightly of our human relationships, in which there is one side who receives and one who gives. The one who receives is never satisfied. The one who gives never tires of giving as long as the relationship lasts. Even in a new relationship, you find the same personalities - the giver and the receiver. There is no lesson to be learnt from this. You cannot change these personalities through training. They will live like this from seven to seventy. Cosmic lessons are always based on worldly lessons and it is not possible to change this aspect of ourselves.

It seems that for as long as the cosmos refrains from re-entering the fires of hell and reshaping itself, existence will keep behaving in the same way; it is waiting for a new hell in order to be able to change. We think that hell is still a long way off. At least, that is what scientists say.

So for now, the prime guiding factor in joining together is becoming steady state, and this is brought about by gravitational force. Atoms, which are charged with negative and positive load through the exchange of electrons, attract each other because of this load. As the bond's ion character increases, their attraction to each other grows stronger and it becomes more difficult to split the relationship. I think this is the reason why sometimes, although we hate each other, our feet cannot manage to carry us somewhere else.

It's not that we are always like that. Some of us share rather than giving and receiving. While atoms connected with an atomic bond are joined by the attraction of oppositely charged ions, atoms joined with a covalent bond connect by sharing their electrons. Water is like this. It shares it's essence. Perhaps that is why when life started out, it chose to form inside water. And separation? The breaking of bonds? What can turn our life upside down more than separation from the friends, lovers and environments we are attached to. We have so many attachments: lovers, family, friends, nationality, sports teams, cultural ties - attachments that hold the different factors of our lives together with tight knots forming a net with which we gather life to us.

The concept known as karma is in fact a 'net' theory. We are in a net that covers the whole cosmos, from subatomic particles to elements, from elements to two million molecules, from molecules to structures. It is thanks to this net that we sense when something important has happened to those we love and the reason why our ears ring when someone is talking about us.
This net might be formed from the traces left behind when energy moves, and for that reason it can only be broken by energy itself.

The elements cannot be broken down except with an energy equal to that which bonded them together. This is different for every different molecule. Some molecules have stronger bonds than others so while a small amount of energy can break a weak bond, only a powerful blast of energy will break a stronger one. As we can see, whether the bonds are in the atomic world or in human society, they do not break apart unless they are subjected to an energy bombardment.
No relationship comes to a happy, contented end, regardless of who has the moral high ground or of whether it is you or your partner that wants to separate, No matter how much a part of us might be relieved at the separation, there is always another part of us in bitter pain.

It doesn't need much further explanation, but be aware that if you enter into a relationship, you will be devastated when it finishes. The stronger the bonds were between you, the greater will be the pain when they are broken. The pain and tension will not be any less, however well-equipped you are to deal with the situation, however well-versed you are in psychology and how ever level-headed you consider yourself to be. The bonds in our life are not just of a romantic nature - the break-up of commercial partnerships can be just as painful.

However much we might wish for a calm separation, you cannot extricate yourself from any bond without being subjected to this pressure and energy. For example, in order for the separation of the water molecule into oxygen and hydrogen, you must either apply an electric current to cause electrolysis or lightning must fall into the water. Commercial partnerships are brought to an end by one partner defrauding the other or establishing a partnership with someone else, or after being subjected to intense energy fields such as economic crises. In one way or another, your heart will bleed as you are engulfed by an exhausting tidal wave of energy and, rightly or wrongly, you will have to endure this process.

You must have figured out by now that every bond is a new formation with which the universe both enriches itself and learns something new. The number of compounds created by the 109 elements that we know of is close to two million, and all are formed with different chemical bond combinations. As an example, the carbon atom is reflected into the universe's mirrors in 1.7 million versions with differing functions and appearances.

Every bond creates its own unique structure, but for some reason or other, seven billion people frame their own personal relationships based on the common structure and outcomes of most other relationships and have these same expectations from their partners. Of course, a bond is a bond; but if we want to understand each other, we need to know what kind of bond we are part of. How meaningful is it to want something that doesn't exist from each other? How strange that despite its futility, we expect things that do not really exist from each other - no wonder we have difficulty communicating. Even those with a good understanding of each other eventually split up when faced with the stress of some untenable request.

We understand the structures of sodium, iron and oxygen, so we don't expect a gas like oxygen from iron, nor that water will harden like platinum. If only we could display the same understanding in our personal relationships. If it is our nature to be flirtatious, what is the point or reality of promising each other a thousand years of sacred commitment? Of course, there is nothing intrinsically problematic with promising commitment to each other and in fact it adds colour to our relationships; but it is problematic to believe in it. Animals do not create havoc in their lives through their relationships. The difference between us and them is that we still do not understand the way things are and cannot stop ourselves from putting each other under pressure. So perhaps we should ask ourselves what animals have that we lack?

Sometimes you can have too much of a good thing. Could the reason for all this be our brain, whose behaviour is dictated by a culture shaped by our social interactions? This is the very brain that we boast of as our greatest endowment. If we agree that the problem lies with our brain, or to put it more conceptually, our mind, how can we find the path to make our mind capable of reaching the depth of understanding necessary for it to deviate from the restricted boxes within which it operates?

Do we need to build a new culture or to be completely liberated from our brains that create the way our minds think? When seeking a solution to this issue, Lao Tsu named the reality he found, 'Tao', which means 'path'. According to Tao, if you liberate yourself from your ego and the impositions of your mind in relation to life, you will see the universe's nameless state. It possesses neither name, shape or sound. It cannot be recognised by our minds. Two thousand years after Lao Tsu, and many miles away in Amsterdam, Baruch de Spinoza construed that the path to correctly understanding life and the universe was through intuition rather than the mind. The two neither knew each other or were aware of their respective philosophies.

We insist that we can't manage it among the myriad of things we have to do every day from dawn until dusk just to earn a living; but no matter how much we have tried to bypass it with the individual and social life models established in the last few thousand years, it is still not possible for us to exist outside of cosmic life. Just as a fish cannot change the sea in which it swims, we too cannot alter the cosmic relationship structure and flow that is engraved into our cosmic memory.

So if that is true, where is this cosmic memory? As the universe proceeds on its path, continually moving and with every subatomic particle constantly dancing, how does it monitor its every step so as to never forget? The carbon atom continues to be carbon and the iron atom continues to be iron. Should we point at ourselves and the brain on our shoulders, as if invoking God, and say that the universe's memory is somewhere on high? Is it here, or are the tracks confused? Is every new phenomenon in the universe a track or mold? Does the universe, which lost its density through cooling and expanding, add new multi-dimensional lines and conceptual capacities to itself every micro-second? As it continues to expand and cool, seemingly without end, will it be impossible for the tracks and molds that formed at the previous temperature to be changed without returning to these former conditions? It would be logical to think so.

In that case, we can presume that as long as the expansion tendency of the cosmos is not reversed, returning to the past and changing life's structure will remain an exciting fantasy that only exists in film scenarios. While the universe has been expanding since its inception to the present day, it has created something new at every stage. Perhaps it will be only after several million years that we will be aware of what is being created today. One day, if the cosmos starts to freeze, we will live our lives from the end to the start, like a film rewinding and perhaps this is the only way to return to the past. Who knows?

Perhaps the cosmic memory does not exist and we are simply surrounded by billion-year ruins, frozen ruins that will thaw again when heated in the fires of hell. Additionally, does the idea of Armageddon as the end of everything originate from the idea that the fires of hell that will slowly consume the universe will melt and eliminate the very tracks and molds on which existence is built? We have no way of knowing. It's just a guess, but the universe's characteristic of molding is like something observed through the window offered by our teachers. Modern education now copies the universe's recall mechanism.

For a long time, we have been learning to read, not by learning letters of the alphabet, but by imprinting word groups into our brains. We learn a second language, not by memorising words, but by absorbing sentences until they are committed to memory. We recognise and know each other from the entirety of our person, not by one individual feature like eyes, nose, clothes or other features, and we appreciate the importance of first impressions. In other words, we assess each other's identities as a whole, not just by seeing how clever, polite, pretty, trendy or good a person is. Additionally, no child only apes the positive qualities of the person they have chosen as a role model. They reflect everything about the person into their soul, the good and the bad. Take for example the type of boy that copies his father in appearing to the outside world as a cultured and sociable person, but also doesn't shy away from hitting his girlfriend from time to time, in the same way that his father treats his mother.

Children perceive and assimilate their school education as a whole, not by breaking it down into single issues. If the child likes physics, they will easily learn all the other subjects. If they don't like physics, even the simplest formula will be unsolvable gobbledegook. Isn't that the same in our human relationships? We love or decline to love on the basis of the whole person. The ugly and negative sides of those we love are both part of the attraction. Can life really be that simple? Or love?

Perhaps the reason why life and the cosmos are so rich lies in the simplicity that stems from the molding process. It would be nigh on impossible to keep that many details of a complex system in the head and maintain it without fault. From that first day right up until today, 14 billion years, the universe's mass has never changed. It has only loosened and, in the process of doing so, spread out. With every new day, a new hue reflected into the mirrors with a new stroke, and so long as it didn't come up against any opposing force, its existence and the details that formed with it were passed on in each new phenomenon.

In fact, the universe made with one hand and deleted with the other. For example, when the electrons and positrons met, there was a fierce battle between the two sides and the main forces of the first cosmic expansion revolution wiped each other out between the glinting swords. You know the rest. Those that remained got together with quarks in the triumvirate period and created atoms.

As can be seen, in the electron-positron battle, the first clash with an opposite deleted all records of itself. Molecules bond, but if they take back the energy they used in coming together they are destroyed. Think of how water suddenly disappears. Salt disappears. The diamond shining on your ring disappears. This is the magic of the universe. If you remove its bonds and tracks, or bring it up against an anti-universe, if such a thing exists, perhaps the universe itself will be annihilated. Magicians perform similar tricks, holding out the wand in their hand and turning it into a frog, or making the object in your hand disappear in a puff of smoke. Maybe all the magician is doing is sending enough energy to turn the object into its reverse. Apart from being used just to point, the wand also serves to make you afraid.

In spite of our communal fascination for magic, societal ethics have a tendency to condemn those who practice or believe in it. Moreover, as it is forbidden by the sacred books, we have not been passed down a large corpus of work on the subject. The reason why the magicians of our legends always live in caves hidden in treacherous mountains must be that as well as being close to the forces of nature, they are able to hide from the soldiers of the king there. It is hardly surprising that kings did not allow any forces that might be able to challenge them. This being the case, the mysteries of magic were whispered like a secret from the master to the disciple and carried on amongst families. Disregarding a few stunning female magicians who star in best-selling novels and a few online wizardry courses, unfortunately we have no other documentation. However, magic is still practised and still yields results.

In fact, magic can be used to many ends. It is extremely widespread and traditional for our mothers and neighbours to seek out the local magician or fortune teller when they want their child's fate to be wedded to a chosen person or want to unravel some other spell. However, no matter how powerful it is, magic is limited by a specific time period. Whether the period in question is one day or one thousand years, at some later time, the spell will fade of its own accord because it is borrowed energy. Sooner or later, the borrowed amount is returned to its origin or the energy drawn from the system is in some way taken back. How?

When the prince kisses the princess who has been asleep for 100 years, she wakes up along with the whole palace. When the princess throws the frog at the wall in anger, it falls to the ground turning into a handsome prince. In both events, the spell was broken by a transfer of energy which is called a counter-spell. This occurrence is somehow similar to the clash of electrons and positrons or the application of sufficient energy to break molecular bonds. It is your choice whether to believe or disbelieve in magic, but there is no need to exaggerate the subject. As we have said, the thing we call magic is in fact a simple thing.

It could be magic that has made it impossible for you to stop thinking about the man or woman you spoke to for just ten minutes last night while out dining with friends. It could even be magic that leads you to rent the tiny flat shown to you by the estate agent, believing it to be the home of your dreams. Let's at least accept that it was magic that caused Barış's teacher to break her leg just before the grammar test he was dreading and that the magic was performed by Barış. To make magic, you primarily need a magician. It could be a professional, but everyone can make magic, including you. The secondary requisite is desire and concentration. This will ensure the energy is sourced and directed appropriately. However, sometimes desire and energy may not be sufficient; in the story of Aslı, the bonds somehow do not form or soon unravel.

Aslı was in the final year of business school. We were in

year two. Along with my closest friend, Aydın, I was crazy about her. We felt as if Aslı looked onto our world from the mysterious depths of another galaxy, thousands of kilometres away. She seemed like someone who hailed from beyond an ocean never sailed by ships. She was unlike us or the others. She seemed to live behind a cloud or curtain. For us, just watching her was like being in prayer. She was tall and slim. Her long, auburn hair flowed from side to side when she moved her head and the sails of my heart were always caught in the breeze.

For some reason or other, although she was often only a few steps or tables away from me, I never managed to pluck up the courage to talk to her. When we finished college, despite all my efforts, I could never find her. It was as if the ground had opened up and swallowed her, or she had returned to the hazy land on the other side of the ocean. Eventually, I began to think that I would never see her again. But 13 years later, I caught sight of her at the new year's party of a new company where I had been working for a year. She had come to Istanbul from the Ankara office to manage a small project.

She was sitting by the window facing onto the Bosphorous, chatting with a thin, middle-aged woman with an intellectual air. I looked into her eyes and said,

'I know you.'

She replied without hesitation. 'I recognise you as well. You're from the Business Faculty...'
She paused and then went on, 'We used to bump into each other a lot.' She looked again very carefully and said, 'But I don't think you were one of the school's leading revolutionaries, were you?'

I laughed and said,

'I was in the spectator's team. I hadn't even undergone my own revolution, let alone take part in any others!'

She laughed as well. Her smile hadn't changed. The line of her lips seemed to carry a little more sadness; but the refined, elegant manner hidden inside her natural beauty was immediately apparent.

'Have you ever thought that it was no coincidence that we bumped into each other so often?' I continued.

She looked at me, then bowed her head slightly, smiling. Then she looked up and held out her glass. Impishly she said, 'Now, let's drink to that.'

Her female companion excused herself and went off to join another group, so we sat down together. I noticed for the first time that Aslı was an incredibly witty woman; as I had never spoken to her at college, I couldn't possibly have known. Her humorous asides, born of a sharp intelligence, were sprinkled almost imperceptibly among the standard conversation and could easily be missed if you weren't paying full attention. Perhaps that was how she measured up the perceptive powers of those she was speaking to. After about an hour, she stopped referring to me using the formal expression for 'you' in Turkish, switching to the more familiar, more personal form. As we swapped stories about our mutual friends, we both knew that there was much else to talk about. I knew that the gossip machine at the office would be in full swing by tomorrow, inventing all sorts of scenarios about us.

I told her about Aydın and that we had both been crazy about her, waiting to glimpse her at the library entrance, but never plucking up enough courage to go in and sit next to her at the table; I related how day and night I had read a famous poem dedicated to a woman called Aslı, although I only learned that her name was Aslı a long time later after I had read the poem countless times. She remembered me from those days but couldn't recall Aydın. After all, our encounters with her were limited to those two second moments when she passed by, or she may have glanced at the two kids sitting at the next table in the canteen. We wanted so much to be close to her but had to make do with watching her from afar. It was as if a magnetic cloud was preventing us from getting any closer to her, but strangely enough it also didn't allow us to stray too far away. In fact, the friend she used to hang out with was also a beautiful woman. It was her bad luck to be at the side of a woman of Aslı's exotic beauty. Aslı's existence was eliminating her chance of being noticed. For some reason, neither Aydın or I had any designs on her friend.

Aslı looked up and straight at me. Her tired eyes looked into mine. She said,

'We might have had very different lives if we had been clumsy one day when leaving the library and bumped into each other. If only you had been braver with me...'

She was about to finish the fourth glass of whisky in front of her. We were no longer shy with each other. It was as if we were trying to fill up the space of a myriad of years. We looked at the glasses then our eyes met. We had come to the point when we both knew what we wanted. I called the waiter and asked for two coffees. Aslı asked for milk with hers. Then, she turned to me saying,

'You should have told me. I had an inkling about you at the time, but it would have been good to know that you two friends shared a love for me.'

To see the embodiment of my silent devotion sitting across from me so many years later was like being in a fairy tale and my feet were far from the ground. Perhaps at midnight the coaches would turn into pumpkins again and I needed to pour out all the secrets I had kept inside me before that time. The things I didn't say would return to where they were before, along with the coaches, and disappear from my life. I had hardly any time. I was the legendary Cinderella. That night, the more she danced, the more I spoke.

Aslı had a spoon in her hand and was tracing small circles with it inside the cup in front of her. The circles slowly grew larger, then shrank gain. It seemed as if she would never stop stirring it. Her eyes were fixed on the coffee in the cup as she absent-mindedly watched her hand movements. Her pupils seemed to mist over and I could no longer see where she was looking but it seemed very deep. I reached out towards her hand on the table and touched her fingers. I was talking, but I couldn't see her, just a silhouette. I felt as if the eyes looking down towards the ground were actually looking at me. Was she listening to me? I couldn't tell but I carried on talking.

It was no coincidence that I had found her, so many years later, when the embers of my feelings still had a warm glow; it could not have been a coincidence. She continued to focus on the cup. The large window looking out onto the Bosphorous had misted over now, along with Aslı's eyes. Now they seemed to reflect the shadow of a deeply buried pain. Who knows what she had been through. She was divorced. Perhaps she had been head over heels in love with him but he had left her for another woman. Perhaps she had been married to a brute who had subjected her to physical violence? At that moment, I didn't have the courage to snap her out of her introspection. It was if she was sitting on a raft, being rocked by the gentle lapping of the water. She was like a song being hummed somewhere deep inside. Then she lifted her head to look straight at me.

'Shall we go up to the terrace?' she asked.

Outside it was getting darker and the chill of the damp evening breeze pierced right through me. Thousands of lights were burning on either side of the Bosphorous. The silhouette of a freight ship was heading towards the Sea of Marmara.

'Do you know,' she said, 'That in the afternoon, all the ships are heading for the Sea of Marmara, and in the evening, they are all travelling from the Sea of Marmara to the Black Sea. If the time is not right, you can't make the right decision; or if you do make it, you can't put it into practice.'

She stopped and stretched out her hand.

'Please hold it. Tomorrow, I am meeting my ex-husband. I'm probably going to let him move back into the house. It's not the right decision - I know that; but it's time for the ships to go to the Black Sea and I can't do anything else.'

I took her hand, saying nothing. Yet there were so many things I could have told her. Life had given permission to start everything unfinished, still connected to where I had left it. I didn't realise that at that point Aslı had wanted me to show courage, and for that reason, she had held out her hand. On the other hand, I withstood the scorches from the flames inside me that wanted to reach her and ducked away from the logical decision. I left her alone. The illogical decisions are the ones that belong to life. Life is illogical; either that, or our human logic cannot grasp its meaning. Life does not ruminate on unpaid household bills: it rushes towards the volcano that is pulling it, so it can burn and be reborn. It chases love. It prepares new gifts for the universe, For life, everything else is meaningless. At that point, I had broken the jade wand that life holds out to us. When Aslı was holding out her hand, life was offering me its jade wand but I was clueless. The bond and the magic were broken.

Now when I think back, for us university students, the 1970s were a battle field reminiscent of the first electron-positron clash. Sometimes, we would say a final farewell to each other before sleeping, not knowing what tomorrow might bring. Just as the electron-positron clouds of that era seemingly did not allow any type of bond to form, there was still a magnetic field between Aslı and I that I could not overcome. During that era, not one of my friends experienced a great romance. Years later in the 1980s, when I heard that the school had turned into something of a love nest, I was happy for the students, but couldn't help feeling a bit resentful at the same time. Our brains, that operated within a system of logic, always left us on the other side of the road. Courage and love are not to do with the brain, but rather belong to instinct.

VOLUME AND DENSITY

When the universe began to expand, it increased in volume and it's homogeneous core diversified. As far as we know, the quarks and electrons became buzzing with tiny tremors. Maybe these tremors were the flurry of our steps towards carry our own responsibility within an unknown process. Nobody and nothing knew anything on any subject - everything was simply buzzing.

Faced with the burden of protecting and maintaining your existence for the first time, and moreover not even really knowing what that meant, you would have no other option than to await the results of yours and other's actions. This is the cause of your tremors. We still tremble when overcome with fear or trepidation. You must remember that. If the tiny particles had some knowledge of God at that time, they might have been comforted to a degree. At the very least, they might have calmed each other by saying ,'May God help you,' from time to time.

Whatever may have happened, it occurred there on an earth that didn't even know its own identity, as our ancestors unconsciously took their steps, albeit somewhat shakily, and began to clash against each other. As a result, the universe for the first time sowed the seeds of an instinct, the survival instinct. As self-defence was discovered, it simultaneously turned into destruction, bringing the end of both sides. The phenomenon we call war is still much the same.

The positrons were wiped out when overwhelmed by the superior numbers of electrons. They became the first extinct species of history, destroyed in the same vein as the Romans who did not leave one stone on top of another in the whole city of Carthage. All that was left behind was a handful of conquering electrons. The electrons could not have known of the attack on Rome by Pyrrhus of Epirus, nor its outcome, just as Pyrrhus himself could not have known of the consequences of this first war. Separated by fourteen billion years, two great armies won two great battles, but they lost everything they had in the process.

During this process, the instincts of a group of quarks were more acute. Although they were clashing, they were also uniting in groups of three, almost as if they wanted to recreate the amity that existed before the big bang. As they held tightly onto each other, generating neutrons and protons, they also began to dance with the lonely, miserable electrons; firstly hydrogen, and then its derivatives and other elements, started to tremble with their new bodies. Existence was cutting out its new suit. Because every element came into being with a different density, they were forced to separate from each other. The universe was imprinting individuality into the earth, like a design. Whatever the conditions, they never lost their attraction to being together. Aren't we all just the same? While independence is one facet of our characters, don't we also pursue union and togetherness?

When one love ends, don't we immediately start to run after the next? When we fight for the ideal of an independent, unbound country, don't we at the same time want our citizens to be connected together and united as one body behind the same ideal? Isn't it the case that we say countries shouldn't meddle in each other's affairs, but also hope for help from international associations? Aren't our clubs, political parties and football teams all adhesives that connect us to each other?

Consequently, as the ever expanding universe grew larger with its merged bodies - referred to by physicists as mass - it began to bend the area around it, or perhaps a more accurate expression would be to say distorted.

The small objects near the masses were dragged towards them by the skewed inclination, causing them to join together and making the mass even larger. Consequently, the distortion that caused the growth increased even further. Physicists call the source of this movement caused by the distortion of the universe 'gravitational force'.

They might not have put it exactly that way, but I think that's what they meant. Scientists identified four main forces. The explanation of the first three was easy, but they couldn't account for the fourth; it was different. It was the gravitational force referred to above and defies explanation. The other three were short range but definitely powerful forces...like electro-magnetic force. They had negative and positive poles which attracted each other, repelling similar poles. Just like we learnt at school. But gravitational force was different. For one thing, it did not carry negative and positive loads, therefore it was not in a position to repel anything. Compared to the others, it was extremely weak, yet despite this, it could reach the furthest corners of the universe. It was like a puzzle or magic spell.

As this force could not work on its own, it needed a transport, and the particle that carried gravitational force was called a 'graviton'. The graviton was massless, but without it the universe would not have been able to stay together. In fact, what we refer to as gravitational force is more a path than a force. A path we made by bending the universe and one that leads to us.

Love is just the same...exactly the same. When it strikes, you don't know what it is. It seems as if you were a normal person until you met the object of your desire, but now you would do anything, no matter how insane, to catch a glimpse and be near them. Is it insanity? In the end there is no need even for insanity... the waters get hold of your raft and take you to its shore.

Gravitational force is inversely proportional to the square of the distance between the centres of two masses. At least, that was Newton's theory. Our fathers were more than aware of Newton's formula when they sent us away to far off countries to null the pangs of love. This method was quite successful. In time, the fires of passion waned and their children calmed down. When the distance between lovers grows, the power of love lessens in inverse proportion to the square of the distance between the lovers.

In other words, the young man who cannot tear himself away from his lover's window is driven by a desire to be close, rather than a desire to see her. For two years, every morning and night on my way out and back home again, I used to stare at the window of Müjgan, who lived a few streets away. For two years, I made sure my route home went down her street. As I got near the door, I would feel pain inside as I waited to see if I could catch a glimpse of her, but I knew that if she had appeared at the door my heart would have stopped. I knew that I only wanted to be close to her, just as the poet Attila Ilhan wrote, 'I'm bound to you.' Everything inside me was pulling me towards her. We had decided to split up, but what chance did decisive words of reason have when drowned in the torrent that flows inside us? She was the not the right person for me and I knew it. She was a liar who denied her lies. I felt like her substitute lover. Now, when I think about her beauty, she was a mediocre looking woman. So what was it that drew me towards her?

It was the same thing that attracted others to her - perhaps it was the power of her will, or her attitude to life. When you look from a mountain to a cloud, you are aware of the difference in density, and it was the same feeling looking at Müjgan. You couldn't help but see the difference between her and others. The intensity of her soul reflected in every direction. Shortly afterwards, she moved to another city. I saw her belongings gathered in front of the house. It was strange, but as I passed her house the next day, I felt as if a load had been lifted from me. In time, the links of the chain that bound my soul to her began to break apart. It was as if she carved her named into wherever she found herself. She was noticed, and her existence seemed to almost give shape to her location.

Physicists say that the more mass increases, the more it distorts its location in space and this causes other masses to move towards it. My father was just such a person. Throughout his whole life, from youth to old age, he was popular with women. And it wasn't just women: colleagues, acquaintances, drifters and bureaucrats all admired him. Drinking at his table always promised an enjoyable evening. In his later life, he couldn't hear very well and could only walk down the street supported by one of us; but he was still the most visited person at the place where he lived.

Before retirement, he was a judge in the High Court. He had made large numbers of convictions and for that reason, he carried a gun with him for a long time. Some evenings, when the stars shone over his table, which was plentifully dressed with accompaniments for the Turkish drink raki, he would sing to his heart's content, stretching out his arms towards the sky as if he had an imaginary gun in his hand and was shooting bullets into the stars. He was a stern man, but even those to whom he gave over 20 year sentences wrote eulogistic poems and sent them to him, writing his name in acrostic form. I once met someone who knew him from 30-40 years ago and hadn't seen him for 30 years. He told me,

'Whenever two people who knew your father come together, they still end up talking about him'.

You can find people like that around you. If you pay a bit of attention, you see them straight away. Any shop they go in immediately fills with customers. They are the most admired people in the office. They don't hold birds in their mouths, but they roam the skies amidst scores of different birds, from eagles to swallows. While the average person tries to conjure up ways to catch the bosses eye to get a promotion, these people get to the top without having to think about it. We see these people as rising stars. The expression 'rising star' is in fact a metaphor, which means that fortune is on their side.

Stars scatter the light they generate around them. However, what really matters is not the light, but the gravitational force of huge masses. In fact, as well as their great mass, some of them have such a great density that the weight of just one cubic centimetre is equal to tons in our worldly measuring system. In addition, they continually grow with the gravitational force of large masses, increasing their gravitational force at the same time. To be a rising star is to have strong gravitational force, just like them; therefore it shows the greatness of your forcefield. Even if you can't always see this forcefield with your eyes, you can sense it - like that of Einstein, Napoleon or Mustafa Kemal Ataturk. They were short people with a small build, but the density of their force was spectacularly different.

Just as a star whose volume is only ten times that of the earth will have a mass density 1000 times greater than earth's density, beneath their unpretentious exterior these people conceal a similar density to one of these stars. Sometimes, rather than speaking of a rising star, we refer to someone simply being 'a star'. We talk of football stars, political stars and music stars. They always have a large entourage with them. Their gravitational fields are so powerful that, no matter how hard they try, they can never be alone. This is the fate of those who are stars. Even if being star is a characteristic that is there from birth, it is sometimes nourished by chance. The things you glean from life enrich you, increasing your density and consequently your mass or force.

If everything in the universe, including even your thoughts and dreams, is derived from the expansion of this initial core, it therefore follows that they will increase our mass and gravitational force. This is why knowledge and skill are crucial. These two factors are the product of millions of years of experience and endeavour; the energy they contain, whilst being mass itself ($E=mc2$), is one of the materials that can enrich us most. It's not just knowledge that counts, but also the love and even hate that is thrown at you. You can add the films you watch, new countries you see, people, friends and everything else, including of course your bank account and money, which is the most refined form of energy over the last few thousand years and therefore a reflection of cosmic mass. You can even add your genetic codes to this list. These are the characteristics that have survived millions of years in challenging conditions and they carry the essence of the energy that has been spent throughout these years.

You don't need to think about why an athletic body, toned muscles and body increase our attractiveness - they are the essence of our energy, carved by nature's trillion-year choices and the reflection of our genetic codes. However, we should never forget that our instincts immediately detect the difference between this and muscles pumped up by performance enhancing drugs or a nose and cheekbones shaped by cosmetic surgery. This is why we should not see it as a contradiction that while women are attracted to strong men, they also find the muscles of body builders comical.

As it's clear, being the centre of attraction is both difficult and easy. We certainly won't be able to change everything through wishing. In fact, anything can be achieved by wishing, but it depends on who is doing the wishing. As long as your inner cosmic mass does not expand, your wishes will unfortunately not have enough gravitational force, in the same way that there is nowhere to accommodate your guests unless you endeavour to finish the building that will house them.

In fact, this is what we mean when we talk of creating a work...creating ourselves. All the things we say we talk of creating - pictures, songs, inventions - are actually the bricks we put in place when constructing the walls of our building. The opposite of this is to be dragged around the gravitational fields of others. We might turn out to be fanatical supporters of a political party or football team, or someone's lifelong slave. Sometimes we don't have the choice, because we have so little and there is little around us. That is fate. Fate is that which cannot be otherwise

HOW FAR?

Until the present day, believing in the words of widely respected scientists has been considered an indication of being in one's right mind. Scientists could change their mind about their theories and propose the opposite of their previous discourse as a new reality, without their own scientific kudos being doubted. So much so that even rumours previously considered to be corrupting society with debased ideas have been incorporated into scientific viewpoints, suddenly promoting discourse to the status of science.

This is why most scientists shy away from illuminating how much the marvellous fantasies of parallel universes or the gravitational force of the hidden 11th dimension might enrich our lives. That doesn't stop us thinking about it and indeed it would be good to do so. It would certainly add colour to our lives to think that we might continue living in a parallel universe after a fatal traffic accident, or to imagine that the secret object of our desires, who we greet everyday but never speak to, might in another universe actually be the partner we are trying to divorce. However, we can't stop ourselves being vexed at the thought of our universe being a computer game developed in another universe.

We might consider the idea of our dreams being the meeting point of parallel universes as a pleasant vision. In quantum physics, something can be both this way and that way. Completely incongruous and irreconcilable features can also come together in complete harmony within dreams, in a way that we do not even find unusual. If our brain can create this harmony as we sleep, it can do the same in real life. In fact, in another dimension, these incongruities can exist nested inside one another without any antagonism. Therefore, your marriage to the partner you divorced can in some way carry on, and you can continue to talk to the friends you have fallen out with.

Our chromosomes drive us to focus on our daily needs to such a degree that we don't notice some of the magical phenomena occurring in life and the universe. Work, food, sex - is there room for anything else in our mind? Therefore, we can only embrace the profound reality of quantum physics in our dreams. Bearing this in mind, rather than dismissing our dreams or leaving them to the interpretations of fortune-tellers, we can use them to guide us to the magical road tucked deep inside our life.

I became acquainted with parallel universes many years ago thanks to a beautiful woman. We generally crossed paths a few times a month at departmental meetings in which the company's financial structure was discussed. When I first saw her, I was surprised that she greeted me as if she knew me well. I thought she must have mixed me up with someone else. In a way, I also felt as if I remembered her, but it was more a feeling of familiarity than actually a memory. We stumbled across each other every break and exchanged chit-chat as we stood sipping our drinks. She was the director of the company that organised the meetings. She was responsible for the complimentary tea and cakes so I thought it was normal for her to mingle amongst the participants. She mostly stood in the corner, monitoring what was going on and quietly issuing instructions to the service staff to ensure there were no hitches. She didn't chat with any of the participants except me. Before long, we began to seek each other out, as if we were committing a petty crime. In the end, she became my reason for going to the meetings. Once she said,

'When I first saw you, I felt as if I knew you from somewhere.'

It was the same for me. It felt as if we had met once in our dreams, but then completely forgotten about it. She was married with a young daughter. My girlfriend was working at the same company. The life choices we had already made were an obstacle to us pursuing anything new. One day, when we were once again together at the meeting, I said,

'If we have another life, let's not leave it so late next time.'

I had opened the secret door. She replied,

'We don't have to wait for another life. Perhaps we are very close in another universe.'

'But I hope not as your brother,' I replied laughing.

'Yes, perhaps we are siblings,' she went on. 'And in yet another universe, you might be my partner...'

We laughed again.

I went on, 'We would have a daughter that looks like you.'

In this life, there would be nothing between us. We both knew that, but it didn't stop us desiring it. However, it was much easier to meet in another life than smash down the structures we had already built and start again. Couldn't it be possible for us to live another parallel life in a different dimension, in the same way that quantum girl can live together with seven different people at the same time in different places? Whether it was actuated through the mind, hysteria or fantasy, it would always be a welcome experience. Besides, in the light of new theories our dreams have been given further weight by the fact that fantasy is scuttling towards the physicists' line.

Scientific realities can be noticed without science. Science is the human brain's intellectual view of life. On the flip side of the coin, the Buddhists' thousand year old theories of life and the universe are so close to the theories developed by physicists in the past 100 or so years that it is easy to mix up who said what. For example, while they say that the emptiness in space is not actually empty, but rather a different form of existence, both sides explain it as seen from their own window.

If physicists see the universe as an inseparable integrity and argue that all forces originate from the same single source, can we say that they are on a different wavelength to Sufi philosophers who ascribe everything to God? Can the Italian friar and philosopher, Giordano Bruno, who believed in the unity of everything that made up the universe and that even God had the same core, or Spinoza, who described all things that created existence as different appearances of the same unity be put on a different platform to our physicists? In essence, even without being a scientist, when you look at life from the correct angle you can see everything. Whether you are looking through the window of wisdom or science, what you will see is almost exactly the same. You might take lessons in physics and chemistry, or theology, or directly from life itself, but in the end they will all come up with the same conclusion.

The universe does not have a separate set of rules for every phenomenon and nor does God... In the olden days, it was said that a blindfolded person holding an elephant's leg would make incorrect presumptions about the animal and wouldn't be able to see it as a whole. However, today we say this idea might be wrong. In fact, you can think that as long as you have allowed yourself to be open, when you touch this book you will understand it and whatever else you touch, its inner matter will flow towards you.

This might be why we touch those we love. Otherwise, what would be the point of so many tender touches to the body with the tips of our fingers? Even if we are not always conscious of the fact that we need to touch to understand, we feel it somewhere deep down within. We feel we have touched heaven with every stroke on our lover's body, because heaven is knowledge itself. There are no question marks there. Everything is lucid and you leave the confines of time to see the past and future as one. For that reason, there is no anxiety or doubt there - existence exists as one and that is the way it is. You don't even need to know, because rather than being a part of existence, knowledge is existence itself. Love is the same. This is why you can feel lost in the infinity of the universe's profound emptiness when making love.

But after a while, the strokes on your lover's body gradually lessen until they completely leave your life. We normally refer to this as getting bored. What does it mean to get bored? Why do we persist in using this meaningless expression that when it comes down to it, doesn't actually explain anything. No, you didn't get bored - you just gathered all the information you needed with your touches. Perhaps you weren't suited to those you met. Who knows? It could be disappointment for example, but it is in no way 'boredom'. That is all there is to it.

FABLES

When life is looked at like this, a fable can be derived from its every detail. Every voice illuminates the meaning of a different word. If it's not possible to touch or listen to life's inner voice, perhaps the most important thing is to sift through the details and simplify it. It is just like undressing - slowly you reach the body and then the heart. This may seem to us as if we are throwing aside its most valuable characteristics, whereas it's not our clothes and skin that are important, but what exists inside. Throughout the universe, the outer surface is a shell. Never settle for what you have seen. If you want to avoid the wrong information leading you down the wrong road, forget what you see first. Colours and shapes can be misleading.

Never forget essences are not found on the surface. Is there any vital organ that lives on the outside of the body? The nucleus of the cell is right in its centre, as is the nucleus of an atom. No country has a capital city on its border. Our vital organs are pretty much in the centre of our bodies. We protect them with our ribcage, muscles and stomach fat, while our arms and legs also serve as a further defence mechanism. Don't question why the brain (cortex) is at the top...it is not a vital organ in the full sense of the word; together with the skull it protects the limbic system in the middle that consists of a few peanut- and walnut-sized pieces. This mini-system at the centre of the skull directs all the other vital organs in our body and takes the role of captain of our bodily ship as it battles with the waves of life's ocean.

The centre of existence is always important. The same applies even in love. Platitudes urging us to look at what is inside rather than superficial beauty might be hard for us to take on board, but one day, in the end, we all learn how true that is, albeit after a few ill-fated relationships. Bank managers who give financial credit on the basis of a company's superficial grandeur cause major eruptions in their own organisation as well as that of the borrower. How many people have been lured into a new job by the promise of leaving behind their tatty old office furniture to work in the gleaming offices of a state-of-the-art building, only to find they have arrived in hell?

Even now, I know that pointing this out won't stop the powerful pull of the outer shimmer. In that case, we have to learn to look properly in order to sort the wood from the trees. First of all you must touch, then open yourself up to take in the information that is being offered to you. If the doors of your soul are shut, your perceptions will be hindered, leading you to the wrong conclusions.

Gravitational force pulls towards the centre of the mass, and the centre is always the densest region. The pressure of gravity squashes the mass into the centre, causing it to densify, and the particles vibrating with the pressure of this density considerably raise the temperature. You can only find out what existence is hiding if you enter inside it. Its exterior is temperate, even cool. The blazing fire is inside it. The world itself is the same; while at one side we are trapped in by snow and warming ourselves at home, on the other we are half-dressed and plunging ourselves into the cool ocean. Surfaces are not a mirror to our interior workings - scorching fires burn at thousands of degrees deep down inside us. It's as if there is a secret psychopath behind the doleful eyes of our planet, and we sense this more when volcanoes suddenly erupt, covering the area around them with molten lava.

While gravitational force allows the formation of a centre in our inner depths, it also hides it, and the density difference that develops in our mass (existence) turns us into two people - our inner and outer... our good and bad side... our virtue and our cruelty. Aren't these the matters that psychiatry wrestles with? In order to find what is hidden in our inner depths, we have to let go in a therapy chair, while our doctor searches for a gap through which to let the lava trapped inside us to flow out. You know that the dense feelings behind our behaviour lay deep down and the face we show to the world rarely reflects our true inner world. Our face is a shallow mimic. We are easily pleased and easily angered. Our face smiles and cries. But our soul stays motionless, deep down in a place that is hard to reach. Just like the difficulty of reaching the depths of our planet; it is in reality impossible and can only be neared.

One day, an employee came to my office and said, 'You know, you're a good person.'

I was surprised. He went on,

'Underneath your harsh exterior is a soft and protective father-figure. So I wanted to wish you happy Father's Day!'

I think he was the only one who had noticed. Discoverers do the same; they try routes that no-one has ever seen or sailed to find the previously unknown.

In order to find reality, we have to dig into the very depths. Therefore, the easy thing is the one that contains the least veracity. The difficult thing is always the one closer to reality, because reality is always deep down. The universe is the same. The common expression, 'easy come, easy go' is true because it refers to the lightest aspects of existence. However, that which is difficult to find or achieve is not easily lost as it is the most tenacious, weighty part of existence, which is always found deep down. When you look over your shoulder, it's still there. It won't be caught in the breeze and fall to the ground like a leaf.

Didn't those relationships we stumbled into easily leave us soon after? Money we came by easily was also swiftly lost. The ton of rocks in your garden puts up a pretty good resistance to avoid being moved elsewhere. For this reason, hard-earned cash is not easily frittered away - not because our miserliness stops us from pulling out the wallet in our pocket. It is heavy. Don't make the mistake of thinking that all money is the same. This is as wrong as the idea that all people are identical to each other. Should the relativity of mass and money be added to the relativity of time? Didn't existence separate out following the Big Bang, develop differently and become independent? Therefore, what could be more natural than everything differentiating itself in its own way?

Fourteen billion years ago, when the one entity broke up and individualised, someone was shouting, but none of us could hear it amidst the clamour.

'Each to their own,' the voice was saying.

The expression has become a cliched saying, but how much does it resemble the universe's formation? If only there was one of us who remembered! At the same time as the one entity was swiftly breaking up, individualising and becoming independent, it was on the other hand grouping together in an attempt to mimic its previous form.

As for life, it stretches and discharges between the sensitive gravitational energy of these two poles. With every compression, life becomes expectant of a new birth and forms the resources for the birth of a new motion. Every motion is a renunciation. It is a gravitation towards freedom by rejecting unity and oneness. Every movement is the release of accumulated energy, and the resulting force shines into our life like the first lights of a sacred day. Movement is the wellspring of freedom and rather than stagnating and accumulating, it loves to scatter and go on its way. The magic charm of freedom is found here: freedom is the face of the universe.

When motion first reverberated in the depths of the cosmos 14 billion years ago, the universe joyfully noticed that it had started changing shape. This was how life made its first steps.

Our quintessence was a profound stillness and silence. On that day, the deep inertia gave birth to motion. Thus, activity individualised existence, creating the essence of life. But activity wearied, and like very ship, it longed to rest in a sheltered harbour.

FORCE AND MOTION

How long can you keep a sailor in a port? How long can you secrete your soul away deep down, by turning your back on the allure of the rising sun. If life yearns recuperation, then that is motion itself. Motion loves to recuperate, but what it actually yearns is the motionless panting of two lovers at the end of a night of passion. When day breaks, the touch of a lover's lips on the cheek starts everything again, once more filling life with sound.

It is curious how much can start and end with a kiss. The princess wakes from her deep sleep with a kiss and sees the prince of her new life gazing at her. The tears pouring down a child's face are dried with a kiss. Everything revolves around it. A kiss is the universe's sacred touch and always ignites magic. Kinesis is the light of the kiss reflected into cosmic space.

When Newton developed his great theory of movement, he most certainly was unaware that the universe had been moving for 14 billion years. He did not know that subatomic particles were trembling non-stop. Even if we think that everything in the universe is suspended in inertia, it is actually running at a frightening speed. That is why, for us, stillness is but the dream of a distant country we left 14 billion years ago. Perhaps our dreams are the evocation of the still wait before the Big Bang, and therefore undisturbed sleep fortifies us for what lays ahead.

Whether you subscribe to Newton's three laws or modern physicists' `Law of Conservation of Energy and Mass', motion is the one of the crucial building blocks of the cosmos. To make something move, you need to apply force. Likewise, to turn an object in a specific direction, force must be applied in that direction. If the force you apply sends the object towards other gravitational fields, the object might head for another mass even if the direction you gave was different. In addition, if the mass is within a gravitational field more powerful than the one you applied, the direction of your applied force might not have any effect.

Besides., if you apply force to an object, it will resist with the same force against you. If you are heading for a fight, your opponent will retaliate, even if you are in the right. Just as the person you scream at will scream back, regardless of who is right or wrong. When you look around, you will notice that thousands of mirrors are reflecting your actions back to you. In actual fact, Newton's laws lucidly explain our societal and individual relationships. Is there any need for further explanation? You can apply the theories above to all aspects of your social interactions. And modern physicists? What do their laws say?

According to the Law of Conservation of Energy and Mass, all types of energy, including mass, can transform into each other but will never disappear. You could also make a fable for lovers out of this law. If your relationship is somehow stuck in a rut, it's only a matter of time before it turns into hate. However, if another channel for love opens out in the meantime, love will flow towards it (it could even be a new love affair). In that situation, from the point of view of The Law of Conservation of Energy and Mass there is little point in us saying, 'How could you have cheated on me?' In fact, the problem is not cheating, but rather the fact that the energy you have built up in your relationship has moved in another direction due to the path being blocked. Taking precautions is fruitless if you don't attach enough importance to the blockage between you. In short, when our relationships get stuck in a rut, we have to choose between a rock and a hard place - either devotion that has turned into hate or a lost lover. As we are not very skilled at approaching the subject with an open heart and solicitude, we are normally not able to turn the energy of our love into a calm and solid friendship relation.

Wealth is the same, once lost it goes elsewhere. The cosmos, which is a closed system, works 24 hours a day, seven days a week, like a table at which poker is being played; one person's loss is another's gain.

This is why, when explaining the law of force related to levers, Archimedes said,

'Give me a stick...and I will move the earth.'

The gigantic universe only moves in accordance with its own laws, which are extremely simple. All you need to do is find an appropriate stick.

Adam Smith's great economics theory is also built on the foundation of universal laws. Using one of existence's most obvious and revealing pieces of knowledge, Smith became the planet's most famous economist of all time. You can do the same. All you need to do is take one of the universe's most simple and straightforward laws (in fact they are all like that) and look at its reflections in life's mirror. Adam Smith questioned why there should be any difference between the principles of societal life and those of natural life. Nature's system could also be applicable to social and economic theories. While pointing out that the value of an object arose from the labour used to produce it, perhaps without even noticing, he was also saying that energy, as a universal value, was reflected in a product through labour.

By saying that thriftiness was a form of delayed consumption, he was pretty much whispering in our ears that money contains an accumulated power and energy. However, as modern theories of the universe were unknown during his lifetime, the findings of Newton's physics were prevalent and subsequently he based his ideas on an incomplete theory of the universe, making it partially erroneous. Smith's starting point was correct, but the theory of the universe he had available to him was deficient. Yet even this modicum of a connection with cosmic life was sufficient to make him the world's most well-known economist, known as the father of classic economics.

In fact, although the conservation of energy law may appear to be simple, it is actually quite confusing to understand. Entropy is a difficult concept to grasp, but it is important to understand it because many believe it is the most important law of physics. The law of thermodynamics states that two systems in communication with each other will find an equilibrium as long as there is no exchange of heat or material-like substance between them. Equilibrium is achieved as a result of a process. It is the point at which two parties have nothing left to either give or take from each other. Equilibrium is the state of equality reached at the end of a process. It is a truce - a laying down of arms.

Perhaps this is why when we are too tired to even lift a finger, we are happy to sit in a corner. Your body has found an equilibrium with the earth on which it is sitting. Seen from this point of view, death, which is seen as a state of salvation and eternal contentment, should be the other name for equilibrium. This is also how it is in war. The battle continues until each side does not have the strength left to fight. The end of the war does not come with victory or defeat. The battle rages as long as the opposing sides are unequal.

The second theory of thermodynamics, and the related principle of entropy, states that isolated materials are more ordered than those that keep together. The warm water that results from the mixing of hot and cold water cannot then of its own accord separate out into hot and cold. Entropy is energy that has lost its capability to function in this way and as long as there is no influence from outside, systems flow from high to low energy. The reason behind this is that systems try to lower their energy level. Electrons want to dispose of their extra kinetic energy and return to their basic energy levels. Atoms vibrate and transmit their excess energy as heat; the flow of this heat travels from hot to cold.

If you have too much energy, you become animated. That could be why we refer to lively people as 'energetic'. Your actions, and therefore your energy, are reflected onto others and energise them. Joy and fury are also a transfer of excess energy; in colloquial language, we say that such feelings and behaviour are contagious. As can be seen, it is not requisite to use physics terminology when describing life. In the law of thermodynamics, all energies transfuse into each other, in the end arriving at a motionless level which occurs regardless of whether or not we adopt these concepts.

Love more or less progresses within this thermodynamic law. But how? Two unconnected people, leading separate, calm lives, known in physics terminology as 'ordered', begin to behave differently once they have met each other. They frequently catch themselves looking at each other, often coming eye to eye and despite their slight discomfort at being caught, they can't stop themselves from doing the same thing over and over again. No matter how weird we know it is, we ask a myriad of potentially ridiculous questions we have never asked a member of the opposite sex before. We talk about our childhood and the streets we used to play in. Then we exchange contact details and talk all night long without ever stopping to look in any other direction. The next day, the email chains begin, then a telephone call and finally, a date. It feels as if there is no end to the things we have to talk about. We don't feel any doubts as we sit talking for hours, gazing into each other's eyes, without even a flicker of boredom.

In the ensuing weeks, the passionate, intensity of the conversation begins to fade. By now we are walking hand in hand. Whenever there is an opportunity - on the bus, train, ferry - we kiss for minutes. But after a while, our desire to kiss everywhere also becomes restricted to a desire to kiss in more secluded places. Before long, we can sit side by side and read a book without feeling the compulsion to touch each other. Then, the vibrations between us slowly begin to lessen and we no longer feel the electricity when our bodies touch each other. The sumptuous pleasure of any morsel of food taken from our lover's fork or plate somehow seems to fade.

As the idea of being glued together seven days a week loses its attraction, we start to remember the old friends we haven't spoken to for ages and call them up to ask if they have forgotten us.
Most of the time, we say that togetherness kills love and this is at least true with regard to the end of the relationship. If you ask how that happens, our response should be that it happens
through the law of entropy. After a period of time, the levels of energies flowing into each other find an equilibrium, causing inertia. The preferred method of avoiding this is to keep your feelings alive with new energy flows from different energy levels. In our social lives, the energy of our friends can help us in this respect. Sometimes, the source of vitality can be injected into a relationship by children, who are seen as a sticking plaster for weary marriages.

We see this same relationship in companies and every type of management structure. Newly arrived managers distribute their accumulated energy around them, leading to extraordinary activity. All the rules and procedures are re-examined and gaps in the product market or other areas of activity are thoroughly researched, while any bad or unproductive practices are corrected. However, after a while the pace of activity slackens off and the organisation turns into a calm sea once again, and no-one bothers to ask why there is an unopened parcel on the desk waiting over a week to be dealt with.

Management experts refer to the point reached at the end of this process as, 'management blindness'. This concept is a sine qua non in Management Science. Once the energy of the company and the manager find their equilibrium, the movement stops. But it is not a necessity to get another new manager in order to get the company moving again. Even new civil service recruits cause a stir around them when they start work. Structures in which everything is questioned and examined are in fact an outer manifestation of energy imbalance. This is why older managers are not keen on new staff and feel uncomfortable with them. Senior staff will always try to rein them in, advising them not to poke their noses into everything.

Pretty much the whole of life exists within the laws of thermodynamics and it is impossible to live contrary to them. After hot and cold systems interact, the molecules' movement stops when they reach the same temperature level, just as togetherness lessens and nullifies the tremors of love. Thus, relationships turn into a stagnant mass in the end. We sometimes describe this as lack of emotion and correctly so, because emotion exists inside a spiritual exchange. If there is no exchange, there is no emotion. Even when you are stroking a cat, hundreds of messages pass between you. If you have nothing to give each other, you have no meaning to each other and consequently, you feel bereft of the sensation known as emotion.

Some physicists believe that the end of the universe will come about through heat death. As the energy differences in the system constantly incline towards finding an equilibrium, the state of balance forms when there is no difference left between the energy levels. This means to be incapable of movement. In the life process we experience as living beings, this is the exhalation of the last breath.

**

When I entered the room, he was sitting on a 3-seater sofa. He waved his hand, inviting me to join him. As I got nearer, he patted the empty space next to him on the right to invite me to sit there, just as he had always done when there was something he wanted to tell me. He had lost a lot of his hearing in the past few years, but when I had suggested trying a different hearing aid, he had replied,

'It's not my ears that have a problem hearing, it's my brain.'

He was 92 years old now...He slapped my knee with his hand, saying, '

Look, my boy!'

He still had a soft, velvet-like complexion, despite a few wrinkles. His long, shapely fingers, that looked as if they had been devised with a ruler, were resting on my knee. I could feel his fingers squeezing my leg. For a while, he was lost in the bustle of the street, then turning to me he said,

'I can't get used to being old.'

The words came as something of a surprise to me and were not at all what I was expecting.

'Everyone speeds past me in the street and I can't walk like I used to. Sometimes, I can't even get up onto a high pavement on my own.'

Near his house, there was a small park where pensioners sat to relax and seek out kindred spirits to chat with. Apparently, a few days before, on his way back from the park, a woman waiting at the bus stop had looked at him, then said loudly to the woman next to her,

'Why do they leave this old man wandering the streets. It's such a pity, they should keep him at home.'

He explained,

'I was so upset. How did I come to this? My rebellion is against old age. It's not that I've got old - it's just that my body has left me to be the brunt of other people's jokes.'

He paused.

'Do you know, when I see myself in the mirror, I spit at my face? Who is that person who ended up in this state, I say to myself. But what can we do? This is our punishment from God. God didn't chase anyone from heaven - heaven is actually our youth. Everyone gets a bitter taste of it. It wasn't just Adam who was chased from heaven, we were all chased one by one. I don't understand why God has such a grudge against us. What did we do that God deemed it necessary to humiliate us so much?'

He took a breath, waving his hand into space as if dismissing any new contemplations as worthless, then carried on,

'An apple was it? Don't make me laugh! I keep thinking about that and I can't find any answers.'

I took his hand and gave it a squeeze, remaining silent. He had worked up until the age of 65. Whilst the years had physically aged him, his inner spark had never waned. To the neighbours, he was now the local 'Uncle Judge '. Not many of his old friends were still alive. He was lonely, but every year when I visited him at public holiday times, he would say,

'Looking forward to seeing you at the next one.'

Every time we said goodbye, the uncertainty of whether or not he would see me again welled up in his eyes and I could feel his wet cheeks as he embraced me. I knew that every parting was for him a reminder of death, another parting. I was to return to Istanbul the following day. I squeezed his hand again. It was soft and warm. We said no more to each other, choosing instead to fix on the passers-by on the road outside. We were looking through the window together for the last time.

Small, doleful partings burn and extinguish all around us just like prototypes of the final, absolute extinction. When Gautama Buddha said, 'Every union disintegrates sooner or later,' perhaps he was referring indirectly to the results of the law of entropy. In other words, entropy is to decrease - to consume in such a way that there is no going back, because the essence of this law is that it is irreversible. No matter how much effort we put into it, how well-intentioned we are and how great our love is, our sacred marriages also weaken and collapse in the manner described by this law. The energy in the system will not be able to regroup and initiate movement again. In other words, after a time, we cannot recreate the love and contentment we once experienced. Revisiting the same room in the same hotel where you spent your honeymoon will not give you the same feeling ten years later. Walking hand in hand along the beach again under the full moon will not recreate the same passionate embraces.

However, we should remember that this law applies to confined systems. As the universe is a confined system, the law explains how the universe will end, working on a universal basis; so to what degree your marriage is also confined will impact on the integrity of the law in your own personal context. The mechanisms of a confined marital bond will collapse rapidly compared to a more open connection in which energy can be refreshed from outside, for example by retaining friendship links and an active social life, going to parties and mixing with others and even some innocent flirting. In this way, your relationship will be invigorated by the energy of external relationships. Bringing other relationships into the mix, even if it just on the level of chit-chat, will kick-start the energy exchange and activate movement in your relationship to some extent.

Even so, it would be wrong to say we have found the secret to saving a marriage. The suggestions above apply to the period of life when you are together. While the energy injected by parties and communal holidays with friends will keep the friendship bond between you and your partner alive a while longer, the sexual relationship is a different matter altogether and this relationship in couples is normally a confined system. Unfortunately, in a closed system the law of entropy is unescapable. In short, even if your sex life has ground to a halt, the energy absorbed from your social connections can prolong your marriage without it becoming oppressive. It might seem like eating a dessert that is just a little lacking in sugar, and one which is eaten for the sake of the children.

When we look at how the law of entropy works, we see that energy flows from the source with excess supplies to the one with less. Heat disperses from hot to cold and any environment with surplus energy moves towards one which is lacking. The person with greater love than another is always the giver. The flow is always from the one with boundless love to the one with lesser quantities or none at all. The opposite cannot be true and the pleasure and pain of love is always felt more acutely by those who love more.

Entropy is the metamorphosis of a decisive condition into an indecisive condition. From the point of view of physics, to be isolated and away from any other interaction is to be in a decisive condition. To mix is to be in an indecisive condition. Looked at like this, we can see that the love relationship is in fact a discomforting and disconcerting situation, but when two mediums come together, who can stop the interaction?

Those seeking love might benefit from a small reminder here. If you are moving into a relationship, aware of how your peace of mind may be upset by it, you should be physically close and open yourself up so that your inner energy can escape towards the other person. For love to pass from your body into the other person, you must get as close as you can to allow the other person's eyes to get as much as possible of the sparkle of your eyes.

There is no return – you cannot reverse either the good or the bad. Once you have made your mistakes, or it has come to an end in some way, there is no chance of wiping the slate clean. The law of entropy is irreversible. It is the very life itself that exists in the universe and there is no eraser made for life. Once love has started, you cannot press delete and go back to the start. Regret does not give you the ability to take back what you have given. Once the arrow of Eros has planted itself in your heart, you cannot remove it; you have no choice but to feel the pain and treat the wound.

REFLECTION OF FORCE

The Law of the Conservation of Energy states that all things can transform into each other and that once we understand this cycle, we can understand life. Turning to the subject of the use of energy, we can say that we can do anything by applying force. Life can be directed by injecting energy into the objects and phenomena around us – only if there is sufficient energy of course.

Put more simply through the microscope of physics, it can be clearly seen that different degrees of energy need to be applied in order to break and crush, or to dissolve, evaporate and fly away. We are faced with similar situations in our social relationships. For example, if your desire for your lover to appreciate you gets out of hand, you can exert strength to make them into a slave, but it won't make you any happier to be harbouring a slave or enemy in the place of a lover. Everything has its own place and proportion. When you lose your head, and sometimes this could be what you want, you can crush the other person to a degree that the result cannot be reversed. When you crush the snail in your garden, you are preventing it from wandering freely and copulating to its heart's content. So when you crush your lover? At the very least, you will turn yourself into an object of hate.

When you apply this repression and restriction to your employees, you can't expect them to be the same people they were before. You will become the manager of injured employees - incapable, uninterested, unable to make decisions on their own and asking constant questions. However, you can be sure that in that state they will never be a candidate for your replacement.
To abuse someone is to directly apply the energy at your disposal to someone else without showing any sympathy.

The person suffers as a result of force. If you wish, you can call this the act of making someone sit on a fire.

Energy, or if you prefer you can call it force, heat, pressure, changes the structure of a matter. It is compelled to change it because an object's mass is increased when it is subjected to energy. The proliferating energy dissolves the bonds inside the object, causing it to take on a new form. This includes chemical bonds. The results vary according to the structure of the atomic bonds. The object might dissipate. For example, when carbon mixes with the oxygen in the air it forms carbon dioxide. On the other hand, it might dissolve, explode, or the molecule bonds might break down and disintegrate. As can be seen, we need to take extreme care before applying any type of energy.

You can't expect to get the same reaction from everyone to whom you shout abuse. Every molecule reacts differently to the energy it receives and you might make a rod for your own back. Jealousy does not intimidate a lover. To shape a tree or rock, you need a hammer and chisel – sometimes applied with every ounce of strength you have and sometimes controlled with delicate care. The force used for the detail must always be light and careful. In order to shape clay, your fingers must apply a gentle force, sometimes wearying from exertion and at other times gliding on the clay as if carried by a summer breeze.

Come what may, you have no other choice than to apply pressure if you want to transform an object into different shapes, and it is the same when it comes to children. If you preach at them and provide them with solutions to everything, you will not teach them anything. Psychologists who suggested this during a certain time period are responsible for establishing generations of family despotisms all across the world. By the time parents realised this, it was too late and their children were no longer children; they were now adults who saw themselves as imperial powers.

Strength can overcome all congestions, but it needs to be applied in the right proportion. An explosion is not required to unblock a pipe – sometimes it is more prudent to replace the pipe. An infelicitous growth must be cut right from the bottom. If not, you will be helping it to survive for eternity by reinforcing its strength. This is why the gardeners secateurs must be merciless. It is for everyone's benefit.

There is also the act of using the energy of third parties or other things – in other words incentivising. This is another form of energy usage, but the energy of other people or things. The force at play in this scenario is gravitational force. We allow the glow of the goal and the taste reflecting from it to draw our child in, leading them off in that direction. This can also be used in your other relationships. It should suffice that the gravitational force aspired to has a lofty goal.

How about money? We have already discussed that and we can consider ourselves familiar with the kind of energy it embodies. Money will doubtlessly change you from the minute it enters your life. If you receive a noteworthy salary increase, you too will change. At the very least, you will be invigorated. Your happiness coefficient will go up and you will be enlivened. Whatever is true for an object subjected to energy, the same is true for you. Bars, clubs, trips, social engagements with friends, parties – they all start to occupy more space in your life. The more substantial the increase in your income is, the greater the changes will be – cosmetic surgery or Botox treatment. Perhaps your wardrobe will be bursting with clothes you have only worn once. Your car and your home may change, and with all probability, your partner too.

What else might happen? Your behaviour could change. As well as the growth in your self-confidence, the impact of your words will also strangely increase. People will be reticent with you, behaving with more respect and politeness. Even as you stroll on the beach in a humble pair of shorts, you will have more of an impact than others, appearing more attractive than other men and women. As is generally said, this is not the inclination to grab some of your wealth or benefit from it in some way, but rather the gravitational force of your energy. You will have no responsibility nor play any role in the changes above, for better or worse. Just as iron melts and changes shape under intense heat, so does your life.

If you like, we can return to thermodynamic law and explore another avenue. The energy that enters your life along with monetary gain instigates extraordinary movement, but eventually the interaction between your energy and the new pecuniary energy will find an equilibrium and bring a halt to the new movement. The reason that the super-rich after a while cease to take any pleasure whatsoever in life and become depressed is not because they have 'a disease' of the rich, but the result of entropy.

So what happens when money is lost? The opposite of course! When the energy and force that you are subjected to is withdrawn, the changes that have been made to the matter/object (your social life) due to intense energy begin to move in the opposite direction. In fact, what is happening is not so much that the energy that has entered your life is taking itself off, but rather that a significant part of it is flowing in another direction. Consequently, your environment will cool and solidify and the solidifying matter will take on yet another new shape determined by its new environment. Then a strange thing happens, if the loss of wealth – cooling-off – happens rapidly, the matter (your social life) solidifies in the shape of your previous lifestyle, as if the loss of wealth has never occurred, and there is an attempt to maintain this previous way of life. There is no money left, but until the credit card and overdraft limits are reached, the banquets and night excursions carry on. Even if the parties are modest compared to before, the drinks cabinet is still replenished with luxury drinks whenever it empties.

What else happens? Family ties become stronger. The iron has hardened and the molecules are keeping a tight hold on each other.

Going beyond all that we have said, money and wealth are not always a good thing and don't necessarily make us more comfortable. You can be crushed by it as it dominates your actions. This gargantuan dependency is not down to the fact that you simply love money; the fact is that money has the better of you, making it impossible for you to just leave it and go. As you get closer to it, the money energy's gravitational force increases until you become glued together. As the wealth grows, so too does your dependency and eventually you cannot free your mind and walk away from it. You are unable to take a long vacation and forget about it. Don't forget that gravitational force is proportional to the size of masses and increases in inverse proportion to the square of the distance between the centres of two masses.

If you went to a planet 100 times larger than Earth, the gravitational force would crush you. Forget going out for a constitutional, you would be stuck to the ground flat as a pancake, just like a character from a cartoon strip. The wealth that you have behind you is no different to the planet on which you live. Mass is mass...and it is the same all over the universe. Those sitting on 30 million dollars are not as free as those that save up 3,000 dollars and go on a trip around the world. Christopher Columbus was the penniless son of a poor Geneva weaver. He became the captain of the King of Spain's ships in a quest to find a route to India. Marco Polo took to the road with his father and uncle in order to deliver a letter sent by Pope Gregorius IX to Kublai Khan. You might even describe him as a postman. Neither of them had a wealth that fettered and bound them.

Nobody throws away a Ferrari – if nothing else, they will sell it and put the money in the bank. It was only after overcoming and leaving behind the gravitational pull of money that Siddharta Gautama became Buddha. Just like the masses of great stars that are a thousand times bigger than Earth, Buddha and those like him possess an enormous energy, which relates to their ability to reject wealth. Siddharta Gautama realised that the gravitational pull of wealth affected his existence and that he would never be free as long as he was under its influence. In order to become Buddha, he had to leave everything behind him.

Coming back to us, when our ancestors used to say, 'Be happy with what you've got,' they were onto something. What could it have been?

THE DIRECTION OF MOVEMENT

Force is the primary motor of movement in the universe. Sometimes we call it energy and sometimes we call it power. Just like the names of God, it is reflected into our life from different angles with a different appearance and name. Force is the essence of everything and consequently it is also the catalyst for changing the essence. Every structure in your environment, has its own unique force helix. The limits of its existence are drawn by the amounts of energy it can take and give. Any exchange of energy that exceeds this will destroy its unique structure. This is why it's so important to use power in a controlled way.

Whilst the arrival of ten million dollars might introduce bold, new colours into the life of one person, it might also wreak havoc on the life of another. In the same way, the pressure you put your child under might successfully lead them in the direction of high achievement, but it could equally turn them into a street yob. We have mentioned it before, but now we are more interested in the power that affects the direction of strength. Force, and consequently movement as well, is linear. It will resist your attempts to change its direction.

You know this only too well. How many times have you managed to change the ideas of your friends? How many times have beautiful, heartfelt words brought back a parting lover? Didn't your attempts to persuade your daughter to go to law school rather than study fine arts turn the home into a battlefield? Which of the logical reasons you gave your son to dissuade him from marrying the unsuitable girl of his dreams made any difference?

The desires and preferences within us are formations that originate and take direction from our inner energy. If you try to change their direction, they resist the new path and begin to exert force in the opposite direction. Apart from seeing this in the decisions and choices that characterise human lifestyles, it is also evident in all organisations, traditions and habits. Every innovation meets with a counter force leading in the opposite direction to the change. In physics, this is called centrifugal force. It is not a different force, although it behaves as if it is different. If you respond to it by treating it as different, it will not be damaging – it's sufficient to understand it.

When my friend Naci decided to hand in his notice, the director initially opposed it. He had been building a good team for seven years; he couldn't just leave and abandon it. Not only that, but who would they find to replace him? There was no suitable replacement for him so he should stay in post. In the end, it was announced to the other staff in the department. Their reaction was even more extreme – some of them were furious at Naci and wouldn't even look him in the eye. All elements of his social relations were resisting to turn round the direction of his work life. How insane was it to leave a high salary and retire at such a young age? The backlash was similar when he decided to get divorced. He was forced to take on, not just his wife, but also his son, father, mother and friends. In their opinion, the worst marriage was better than being a bachelor. In any case, there was no need to derail a moving train.

Two steps away from homelessness, Suleyman had taken a beating from his father because of his decision to leave home. Then his father had left for work, firmly closing the door to him. No doubt the three men who used to gather in the park every evening to search the bins for any usable contents and drink the wine they had bought with their last few coins had met with a similar fate that had taken their lives onto the streets. Hidden away in the depths of their past was a man who had tried in vain to influence their direction and resist them leaving home.

The day after his decision to resign, Naci went again to see the director, this time reassuring him that he would remain in post as long as was necessary, but making it clear that a replacement would have to be found as this wouldn't go on forever. He took his foot off the accelerator. He was going into a bend and had to slow down in order to counteract the counter-directional force, because however much he increased his speed, the force pulling him in the other direction would increase along with it. In addition, as the pain of the new route towards the old one became more acute, it would strengthen the forces opposing it.

Following this, he took his boss and colleagues to his side, one by one, to explain his reasons and why he was forced to take such a decision. By doing this, he was laying the necessary filling, breaking the impact of the bend with adverse camber. After this, everything immediately calmed down. He was still the man who had made a decision that would turn the company upside down and in reality nothing had changed. Nevertheless, the force pulling him in the opposite direction had been neutralised.

Reforms in society also meet with a similar counterforce and most reformists are removed before they get to see the fruits of the changes they have set in motion. Just like cars at the side of the road that have overturned after miscalculating the bend, you can see similar wreckage in the wake of every reform movement. How about revolutions? Revolutions must navigate sharper bends than reforms and they always race headlong into them. Counter revolution is the greatest threat to a revolution and always follows in its path. It may or may not succeed, but every revolution must tussle with its protagonists. For this reason, it is critical that the conditions are ripe for a revolution. It could be that Karl Marx did not apply the laws of physics when he foresaw that socialist revolution would occur in the last phase of capitalism, but like every great thinker, he had a good sense of reality. If the working class and the mass of their tools of production did not build the required camber for the great revolutionary bend, the revolutionary vehicle of change would be overturned by the force coming in the opposite direction. Beneath all unsuccessful movements for change lays an inadequate infrastructure or support.

Perhaps this also explains the pernicious fate of the Soviet Revolution stemmed from this and the fact that Cuba is on the edge of poverty and deprivation. The notable point here is that when the revolutionary vehicle fails to slow down, it continues in a direction similar to the forces of the old regime in order to avert overturning at the bend. With the revolutionary direction changed, repression and dictatorship became the manifestation of workers' power and we were fooled into believing it. Yet the initial direction of the vehicle was towards a regime for the common good, equality and freedom for all.

That's the way it goes sometimes. You make a revolution and afterwards ask yourself what, if anything, has actually changed. Most of the time, this question is lost in the clamour of the revolutionary explosion, disparaged and forgotten about like a tiny spider hanging delicately from the ceiling...until someone reminds us again. George Orwell whispered the real fate of the Soviet Revolution into our ears by writing his book, Animal Farm.

Every change in course triggers an opposing force. As we said earlier, these forces are not really opposing forces, but rather the power of movement contained within the old course. Indeed, our own past wrestles with every new aspect that enters our life. The greatest enemy of every new development is its own past: the enemy of capitalism was its economic forerunner, feudal society; socialism is the enemy of capitalism; nationalism is the enemy of internationalism and, although it may not interest you, long skirts are the enemies of the mini-skirt, in the same way that the swimsuit is the enemy of the bikini.

In public, you might defend the right of partners to their freedom, but you oppose your husband or wife going out on their own at night to hang out in bars. What's important is your personal life experience, not what you feel about other people's lives. Even if the institution of marriage is contrary to your intellectual ideas, you are not able to reject it and sparks start to fly when your wife returns from a night out, drunkenly carrying her shoes in her hand. These sparks are not connected to your beliefs, but are a reflection of the force that has maintained your marriage for years caught in your mirrors. If you were completely alone in the universe, moving in line with your one single choice and had never thought of changing it, the flow of your life would continue in the direction of this first choice, without altering course.

Route changes always set you on a collision course, leaving you with no choice but than to fight against your current life and the forces that convey it. The same is true whether you decide to change your job, partner or place of residence. Remembering that those who know the laws of physics understand everything, we know the road to success is illuminated by knowing which force to apply to which degree and where. This will also prevent your life from being derailed by unnecessary accidents.

However, we should bear in mind that our universe is distorted, so it would still slowly alter the course of our linear movements even if there were no opposing forces distorting our trajectories. We now know the reason why: no phenomenon is completely linear and even the cleanest line we can draw will curve in keeping with the universe. This is why our ideas and behaviours gradually change shape. Maturation is to live the requisite duration of time. After this duration, we see the curved shape of our linear line on its cosmic path. Maturation is the visible completion of the process formed by differentiation (camber).

So where is the consciousness we so hotly pursue taking us and how much can it help us to perceive the universe? The current shape of our bodies is about 500,000 years old. In this time period, our chin has shrunk somewhat, our forehead has widened and our hair must have diminished. This is as much as we could manage. When it comes to the brain cortex, it was only able to master writing 5,000 years ago and still does unfathomable things. I wonder if humans got a little too full of themselves when they learned to read and write, or if these hare-brained acts come about because the brain cannot overcome our malicious impulses?

We cannot stop fighting each other, even when our stomachs are full. It is not the hungry poor who sound the clarion for war, but affluent rulers. Furthermore, the poor do not follow in step with passive willingness, but rather enthusiastically support it. Two thousand four hundred years ago, we sentenced the great Socrates to death for denying the existence of God, although we were good enough to administer him with hemlock to save him from a long, painful death. Eight hundred centuries after that, with the blessing and leadership of Bishop Cyril of Alexandria, we stoned to death the Alexandrian mathematician and astronomer, Hypatia, declaring that educated women were witches. However, that was not enough and we felt the need to drag her body through the streets and set it on fire.

The establishment of the notorious inquisition courts is less than a thousand years ago. According to some sources, over 50,000 people were tortured to death in the witch hunts that took place from the 15th to the end of the 18th century. Before we leave the topic of torture, we should note the fact that it is an act we have accomplished with great skill throughout all periods of our history: we have caused organ explosion by forcing water down the throat; we have crushed our fellow human beings in a press until their bones broke, followed by their other organs; we have buried people alive; we have tied their legs and arms to four horses then pulled them until their bodies came apart and we have burnt them alive. While some of us carried out these acts, other of us watched. Curiously, we pursued these excruciating tortures with a humanitarian zeal, believing we were saving the victim's soul from Satan before they died.

Four hundred years ago, Giordano Bruno, who said, 'Divinity reveals itself in all things,', was burned alive in the Compo de Fiori in Rome, after being subjected to great torture. If only we could say, 'Yes, but that was centuries ago.' But steam trains began operating only 20-30 years after the end of the inquisition and just 100 years later, we began to light our houses with electric bulbs. We might derive comfort from the fact that in 1920 the Vatican apologised and canonised Joan of Arc for burning her alive as a witch, but just 20-25 years after this, on the eve of the atom bomb's arrival, we sent six million Jews to their deaths in purpose-built murder factories. War between states is not part of the subject, because the focus is on brutalities we have inflicted on the neighbours with which we have lived side-by-side. Most of the examples above occurred in the last 500 years of the last 500,000 years in which we have lived in societies.

Is it over now? Unfortunately not, unthinkable tortures still take place in prisons, supposedly to extract the truth and aid the pursuit of justice. In some societies, men and women are buried in the ground and stoned to death for adultery. Moreover, the stones are thrown by the neighbours you drink coffee with every morning, or by the family of the baker who you buy bread from every evening. Not to mention that just 18 years before this book was written, in 100 days starting from 6 April 1994, 800,000 Tutsis were slaughtered by the cleavers of Hutus in Rwanda. Don't even ask why UN peacekeeping forces withdrew during the massacre nor why our developed nations effectively rendered the UN a functionless organisation.

I think that it may take a few more billions of years before consciousness matures in the universal sense. We don't know whether the human race will withstand this period, but there is no harm in hoping. Like every motion when it starts out, our consciousness will follow a linear path and everything that forms within it, be it right or wrong, will scrupulously conform to universal laws, whatever else may happen along the way. Its acquiescence will expand, just as iron expands with heat and tightens when cooled. When directed towards the new, it will be constricted by the forces of the old. Life will be the same too and we will see our experiences in this way through the mirror of our consciousness. But within time, as it proceeds down its path, our consciousness will alter within the arc of time; perhaps three billion years later we will be able to see this change clearly. When that moment comes, maybe a human with qualities we cannot yet even conceive of will wave to us from the depths of the cosmos. First of all, we will hardly recognise the person, but then we will hesitantly raise our hand to return the greeting like the frightened flutter of a wing, saying, 'My God, what a change!'

Can we know how far the chain formed by the links of life will stretch? We cannot know, but we do know that life is a chain. Whichever way you look at it, the light of a different link is reflected in life's every face. Did we say that the cosmos seeks unity and that the ticking of time, as the only adhesive and placeholder of the cosmos's unity, joins up every step with its hooks, thereby creating history? Even if we didn't exactly put it that way, I think that's what we meant. History is our entirety reflected into our consciousness, swaddling all life like the fine loops of a lace border. Perhaps the loops are actually the arms stretched out by the universe to protect itself.

Existence wants to be unified again and is fighting back. We want to recapture the genie that escaped from the lamp, but it isn't possible to resist the process that removed the genie from the lamp. We want to come together and be as one, yet in the next breath we are once more reproducing and scattering. While love propels our bodies and souls into the same cubicle, its seed also creates new bodies, separating our bodies and souls again and propelling them away from our merging mass. Just as we find we have something we want to hold onto, everything slips away and we are thrust forward once more. Rabbits and hounds are always caught in the chase. Samsara, which is said to be the circle of birth and death, keeps joining up the links of causality with a karmic presence. Maybe this life, which we say is a cycle of life and death, is no different to the fate of Prometheus.

Every force is another face of the cosmos. So who knows, perhaps gravitational force is the scream of dispersing existence and that is the reason for our bond with the past. That is why the spirit of our ancestors always pulls us towards them and we hear them whisper in our ears,

'Don't lose your bond.'

It could explain why the past is important in our personal and communal life. Our existence is played out on its stage and our memories are most sacred, sometimes even of an equal value to existence. They are its meaning. Perhaps gravitational force is existence's resistance to karma. As the wheel of karma turns, life chips at our existence with endless taps, like the beak of a woodpecker. Life tears down what it has constructed and rebuilds it, while time, which is life's memory, never stops, like the crank of a millstone. If it wasn't for the ticking, time would not progress and existence would not disintegrate. The striking of time gives the rhythm of life. The beat of our heart is the same...

Resonance is the dissolver of wholeness. When the endlessly repeated oscillations become equal to the natural frequency of life, existence cannot stand up to the growing magnitude and breaks down into pieces. This oscillation is the start of the magnitude's progression towards eternity. Eternity is beyond existence and destroys it. For this reason, it is not feasible for the fairy tale prince and princess to live happily ever after all their wishes have come true. This is why all routine activity results in boredom and, whether we are lovers or married couples, experts recommend us to introduce new aspects to our lives in order to prevent resonance. Just as you are infuriated by your husband always kissing you in the same place, so too will the same cry you release in the same position eventually start to annoy him although in the early days it filled him with pleasure.

Anything that turns into a routine is destined for the same fate. Forget the balancing of frequencies, all kinds of equalisation give rise to the same result, which is destructive. To balance is to come to an end. After many years of marriage, when a husband and wife start to resemble each other and even give the same responses, the magic of the relationship comes to an end, leaving the bond exposed to the corrosive effect of the wind.

If all races ended in a draw, no-one would want to go and watch and nor would the competitors be bothered to run. If the weather was the same temperature everywhere, there would be no wind, the fruit would not be inseminated and the grain pods would be empty. Equilibrium and inertia spell the end of life.

When we used to dance together, I would feel her surrendering her entire body and soul to me, so that I knew which step she would take in which direction from the pulsing of her body> She would almost fly in my arms as if carried by a breeze. We never asked each other what we wanted when we were dancing or making love; we were like a river cascading down a waterfall and a twig carried along in it. One of us was the bubbling river and the other the twig making its journey within it. At times, we were completely silent and on other occasions words we could hardly distinguish would flow from our mouths like the words of a song. Whenever one of us called, the other would drop whatever they were doing and run to the other's side, without even questioning why they hadn't called for the past few days. We could gaze into each other's eyes for hours, without feeling the need to utter even one word. I used to watch the way her fingers fidgeted on her teacup and be overwhelmed by the light reflecting from her eyes. She used to say that when I was looking at her hands, a rush of emotion would course through her entire body, starting from her fingertips, and that she would tremble as if we were connected by an electric cable.

We never thought about being equal in our relationship. If anything, that was the last thing on our minds and we never stopped to wonder whose personality was the more dominant. We just ran to each other whenever we found a moment to spend together. She sometimes came to my office and would sit lost in thought, watching her fingertips dance on the porcelain cup. Our connection was the connection of wind, water, torrents, waves and phosphorous. When I told a female soulmate, she began her evaluation with, 'That's good – you've both become sex slaves.' She couldn't comprehend, as her mind only grasped the type of relationship with designated cultural roles. In the mind of my friend, the way to show how much we valued each other was through spending money and she therefore judged our relationship to be only about sex. As well as that, in her mind sexuality was a bad thing.

However, this love did not require holidays in touristic resorts or the red sparkle of a fine wine in a luxury restaurant to make it flow. It was simply the love of two bodies and two souls flowing into each other. Love's only requisite was to leave the gate open – after that it would follow its course. Just like unplugging an electric cable from its isolation switch, as long as you cannot lay aside the shields of your soul and ego, the gate will always be closed. When you opened the gate to release the magic charm inside you, it found the other gate and began to flow in accordance with thermodynamic laws. When the flow started, you forgot everything you had been told about life and just become an extension of its spirit.

From that moment on, you can see without looking and feel without touching. At this new gate, you can be a slave to the other person, even drink the most viscous poison from their hand. Every time you touch them, you can be catapulted into a cosmic journey to the furthest corners of the universe. But thermodynamics is a finite law and once the flow stops, you will see that the tremors of your life leave your soul – but you know that now.

DANCE OF SHIVA

Perhaps there was no need to write so much. In the legends of the Hindu divinities, everything is explained in great simplicity.

This is what they say:

At the beginning, when there was nothing, there was a small egg, which contained the entire universe. The ground, sky and anything else that existed were no different from each other and everywhere was in darkness. Then, this shapeless egg was broken and part of it became the sky, while the other part became the ground and began to expand. The universe was continually disappearing and being reborn in an eternal cycle of creation and collapse, and every time the god Brahma would appear from the mirror of the god Vishnu and break the egg to start everything again. Every part of Brahma's body would turn into living creatures. Following this, the goddess Shiva would appear in Vishnu's mirror and destroy life.

Vishnu, Brahma and Shiva are three reflections of the dynamic of the universe in the divine mirror. They are different faces of the forces inside existence and continually transform into each other. Shiva, who is the most explicit image of divine force, has five divine characteristics and actually represents the law of thermodynamics and entropy. Shiva turns the universe into a fireball, blights everything and brings an end to life by turning everywhere into a desert. As the gods die along with living creatures, Shiva turns into Vishnu again and drifts into sleep along with the universe. One stage of the last act is incredibly reminiscent of the heat death of the universe, which is envisaged by the law of entropy.

As well as this, it is as if Vishnu's transformation into three gods stresses the unity of universal forces and is a guide for physicists researching 'The Theory of Everything'.

Shiva is not just destructive, she is also a transformative goddess of life and death, and her dance is the endless transformation of birth and life. She is the queen of dance, and her movements give the universe its rhythm. Motion exists with her dance, and life vibrates with it. The dance of Shiva is the dance of subatomic particles and life's rhythm and harmony exist through it. Perhaps this is why there is a two-metre high bronze statue of Shiva, dancing inside flames, in the CERN institute. Why else would there be a statue of Shiva at the European Organisation for Nuclear Research, which researches the beginning of the universe with its large hadron collider?

Gautama Buddha likened nirvana to the extinguishing of a flame. The law of entropy, which explains disintegration and expiration, indicates that existence's final goal is one and the same. While Buddha talked about unshakeable happiness, he also explained that this happiness leads to eternity. According to his ideas, our home should collapse and our existence should reach total expiry. This is entropy nullifying life's flowing energy and reaching motionlessness at the last point of equilibrium.

As for karma, it is not an individual action, but rather the motion of the universe, which will not come to a bitter end unless it stops. Buddha succeeded today in reaching the balance we are to reach at the end of universal life. This was nirvana – eternal inertia and death - a place where life is motionless.

The goddess Shiva, with fire in one hand and the drum of time in the other, was dancing ceaselessly with her four arms. The entire universe would dance with her until she stopped and fell into her deep sleep. With her sexuality and hermaphrodite character, she created and celebrated the motion of existence. She was the never-ending life and death cycle of the universe, which would constantly start over and over again.

When we close our eyes and give in to the flow of life, along to the rhythm of Shiva's drum, we experience love, war, defeat, victory, rebellion and death. While neutrons, protons and quarks traverse the depths of the universe with us, the universe continues along its road, ever expanding to the same rhythm. As for us, while we look into each other's eyes and touch in a trance, in a far off corner of our dreams we are walking towards the last sleep of Shiva.